MY WORD

MY WORD
Christian Preaching Today

HOWARD WILLIAMS

SCM PRESS LTD

FOR

BRONWEN *and* GARETH

HUW *and* GWILYM

who want the last word

334 01060 8

First published 1973
by SCM Press Ltd
56 Bloomsbury Street London

Printed in Great Britain by
Cox & Wyman Ltd
London, Fakenham and Reading

Contents

Preface

I have written this book for those who try to speak about the faith in a swiftly changing world. It is a part of wisdom that we should not be blind to the things that change nor insensitive to the ways that abide.

The preacher, like the author, speaks not for himself alone. He draws from many sources and without them his tongue is dry.

It will be clear that I am indebted to the world of scholarship, on which we all rely. But I am also indebted to those who first told me the story and to the ones at home who have given so much understanding to a work that many regard as strange and some count to be absurd.

I am grateful to Barbara Stanford, who typed my script and who sustains much of the work at Bloomsbury while I am offering the word.

I am content with a word from Pascal: 'Certain authors, speaking of their works, say "my book", "my commentary" . . . They would do better to say "our book", "our commentary", because there is in them usually more of other people's than their own.'

Bloomsbury Central Baptist Church
August 1973

1

The Sermon is Out

Until a few years ago it was the custom of *The Sunday Times* and *The Observer* to give some little space advertising the Sunday services of a number of London churches. This was a courtesy which had been offered over many years. It was done, as far as one can judge, without favour to any particular denomination. It was simply assumed that certain churches could expect a visiting congregation and that it would be helpful if people knew the times of the services and the names of the presiding ministers and preachers.

In time a letter was sent from the office of one of these newspapers to the ministers of the selected churches, followed in a day or so by another letter from the other. I forget, now, which came first and I do not wish to press the claims of either newspaper as being the forerunner in the message they gave. It was pointed out that the increasing demands for news-space now made it impossible for them to offer this service any longer. We were reminded that the service had been given for many years and we were invited to accept the deep regret with which this decision had been reached. In turn the ministers replied in a civilized way expressing thanks for what had been received and sorrow that circumstances made this impossible in the future.

The Sunday Times and *The Observer* now advertise as an alternative some guidance about where people can go on a Sunday in London. I am not sure whether the new arrangement is more profitable. This, however, is of little significance to the point I am making – the change was made on grounds of space and not expense. The visitor to London is now offered a catholic and varied programme. Exhibitions, gardens (involving some slight travel and exercise), music, open air events, theatrical events, walks and pub crawls. A generous mind will recognize that there is some attempt to cater for everyone – or nearly everyone, for strangely there is, so far as I have observed, no mention of a place of worship except for a few 'special' occasions. This is a slight exaggeration for I recall that people have been invited to meet, at a particular time, so that they could inspect a church building of some architectural interest. There is a similar arrangement in Moscow for visiting famous church buildings but you may turn the pages of *Pravda* in vain for some guidance about times and places of worship.

I have been encouraged in this meditation by two of our serious newspapers. They claim not to indulge in the superficial and trivial and sometimes it is asserted that a wayfaring man may easily recognize the kind of person who reads them. Are we then to assume, in 1973, that the people in London on any Sunday would not dream of looking for a place of worship? I am not good on statistics and am inclined to view an obsession with them, on such a subject as worship, as bordering on satanic anxiety. But it is clear even in these benighted days that there are tens of thousands of people who are offering their worship in Christian churches in London on any Sunday. Indeed there are more people meeting with serious purpose in the churches than anywhere else in the city. Such devotion will not receive the approval of all but one has a right to hope that it will be welcomed by some.

Strangely, the decision of the two Sunday newspapers, which I have used as a parable, will gain the support of many Christians. This is partly born out of an eagerness to display a proper secular mind. I am not now thinking of whether in fact the newspapers could have been expected to continue announcing the services. I am thinking rather of the zeal of some Christians for self-destruction under the mistaken impression that they are engaged in a worthy form of self-sacrifice. It is, I suppose, the pressures of sociological change which make people ready to get rid of something which is traditional, however valuable, simply because it is old. To such minds the appearance of 'success' is in itself a condemnation. A church which is well attended is somehow seen to hold back the radical advance which could be made if it were not there. It is assumed, contrary to all evidence, that if such a church were broken into fragments then there would be a large number of house-groups or other similar enterprises which would present a far more living witness. Much the same argument is used about buildings themselves. Vital Christian ministers rush to sponsor the sale of church buildings ostensibly, of course, for the sake of the poor. Usually they have no responsibility for these buildings and their zeal is of the sort which would sacrifice the property of others. I have noticed, too, that when their own responsibility is challenged about buildings for which they should have some care they are swift to change their minds.

Now it may readily be agreed that there are redundant church buildings. It would be strange if this were not so in a generation which emerged from a period when there was a fever of church building. A century and more ago all over Britain the people were feverishly putting up buildings for worship because there was a need for them. Times have changed so swiftly that buildings which were vigorously used so short a time ago have now outlived their usefulness. It is one thing to recognize this change, which was brought about by a variety of influences, but it is quite another to assume that because this is true of some – even though they be many – it is necessarily true of all. A little observation will make it clear that this is manifestly not the case.

The reason for the peculiar joy with which enlightened Christians greet the closing of churches and the wilting of membership goes much deeper. It is to be found in the claimed disenchantment with what goes on in the buildings. There is still a warm shining-eyed approval if the buildings are used for acceptable social work. Where this happens there is presumably a service given to the community of which the most secular mind must approve. The rub comes regarding those activities which are traditionally and by belief associated with churches. It must be understood that whatever activities may be listed on the notice boards of energetic churches the real activity of the church may be summed up in word and sacraments, however these may be interpreted. Buildings which through centuries have been used for a surprising variety of communal activities are marked by their structure and by public understanding as places where the word is preached and the Sacraments are celebrated. Where the witness of the human voice has been muted church buildings still speak with stone mouths. So Solzhenitsyn, for example, has heard the stones cry out proclaiming the word in Christ: 'People were always selfish and often unkind. But the evening chimes used to ring out, floating over villages, field and woods. Reminding men that they must abandon the trivial concerns of this world and give time and thought to eternity ... Our forefathers put all that was finest in themselves, all their understanding of life into these stones, into these bell-towers.'[1] You may be sure that Solzhenitsyn was not remembering any common social events in these words. He was celebrating the faith.

I am sure that many church buildings are not adequately used, but I am simply making the point that however popular they may be as a meeting place for the people there is one thing needful which must not be neglected. They stand as a sign and symbol of the heart of the Christian faith and this has been their character throughout history. As a Baptist I was nurtured in the faith in a tiny village chapel. It was like a house but bigger because it was the meeting place of the people of God especially for times of worship. This did not mean that the celebration was limited to the building. When the service was over the door was locked and the people were expected to live their faith at home and at work. When the 'family' met again the doors were opened. I can see nothing perverse or strange about this. Yet I have heard noble-minded people lament a building for Sunday worship simply because it is used so infrequently. These same people are able to accept the festival fortnight at Wimbledon, the occasional summer activities at Lord's Cricket ground or the winter battles on Arsenal football ground as a divinely protected right. Any one of these sacred turfs would be an admirable setting for old people's flats – with all that space!

I take it, then, that a church building would normally be

used for preaching and the sacraments whatever other uses would seem helpful in different places. If another building is used for this purpose it would presumably be prepared for the occasion. And if there are symbols inside it seems rather pointless not to have a sign outside. That is, if it were preaching then there would be a place from which the person could speak and it would seem desirable that he should be both seen and heard. Similarly, if it were communion or the Lord's Supper then there would be a table for the bread and wine. Infant baptism would need a basin for water but believers' baptism presents peculiar difficulties and I can hardly imagine a communal secular building providing a baptistry for this purpose. I have noticed that groups of Christians who are rather proud that they do not spend money on buildings are glad to have the chance of using ours. But if the real question is about the worth in worship then it matters little whether we are talking about a traditional church building, a chapel, or about a building adapted for this purpose when the need arises. Is the faith to be celebrated through Word and Sacraments or is there some other way in which the witness is to be continued or none at all?

From time to time we shall refer to the act of worship in which the word is proclaimed, but my concern is not so much with worship as with the sermon and preaching. Not that we can assume worship is accepted as a way of life by the majority of people; but there are Christians who feel no need of a sermon at all and frequently view it as a hindrance to worship rather than a help. Traditionally the Quakers have given the impression that it is best to have worship without a set sermon, although in some of their meeting places they have made provision for it. There is certainly a strong esoteric attraction for the spiritually-minded in the silence of a Quaker meeting, but this does not necessarily mean the absence of the spoken word. Men and women who feel moved to speak do so, and sometimes this can be an enriching experience as I know from my days in the Leeds Meeting House of Edmund Harvey, who was MP for the Combined Universities, and his brother John, who was Professor of Philosophy at Leeds University. Yet an unwitting reliance upon gifted extemporaneous speakers holds its own peculiar peril. It is not without significance also that the organizers of a broadcast Quaker service felt it would be expedient to help the Holy Spirit by prompting the participants beforehand. Still, on the whole, Quakers have given the impression that the sermon is not a thing to be coveted.

This resistance to the sermon and reaction against its place, historically, in Christian worship has become more marked in recent years. There has been, for example, a growing criticism of the pulpit and its alleged position six feet above contradiction. Since this quip is used by bishops – playfully when they are off duty – and atheists, indiscriminately, it will be well to give it more attention than it appears to deserve. I must confess that I have not been aware of any profound difference between speaking from an elevated pulpit and addressing an audience in a university lecture hall where frequently the speaker is low and the audience uplifted in a rising semi-circle. Indeed the lecture hall seems psychologically more dangerous with its temptation to assume an intellectual superiority. It is interesting that both lecturing and preaching have become pejorative words and this would suggest that any attempt to speak to others, from any position, is a hazardous experience. In common speech we hear expressions like: 'Of course, I don't want to preach at you' or, from the other side, 'Don't you start preaching at me.' The implication is that people do not wish to be accused of scolding or fault-finding speech, and that no one likes to be exposed to it.

There must be, alas, some reason for such a common use of the word. Occasionally I have endured this activity from the pulpit myself but I find it much more of a habit in other spheres of life. Policemen, for example, where the gently remonstrating, 'Hullo, Hullo, Hullo . . .' has descended (or risen) to 'Where the hell do you think you are going?' Magistrates with elongated forefingers tell people how they ought to behave as though their own lives were above reproach. Politicians indulge in endless criticism of opponents for sins which nestle in their own minds. Trade-unionists complain about employers and management and these in turn scold the workers. In such ways is preaching, in a pejorative sense, the most common form of human speech.

Yet why is it that preaching, which was a new language created within the church, has been chosen to describe what we all claim to deplore even while indulging in it? Here I think the 'pulpit' itself must bear some blame. Set up as a place from which a man expounded the 'word of God' and offered the gospel it has appeared in all shapes and sizes. Simple wood pulpits built for utility; wide histrionic pulpits encouraging a man to orate; pulpits like boxes and pulpits like palaces. When the decision was made that there should be a place from which a man would preach there were all kinds of architectural extravagances and distortions. This uncovers a not uncommon excess among architects, for they have done the same with houses and public buildings. If the mood and time demands something proud and pompous then they will readily provide it. If the request is for something beautiful or modestly simple then this may be provided too. The story told by pulpits reveals a great deal about changing theological thought through centuries of time. Indeed, pulpits like tables and altars portray the way in which a people understand the God they worship. Yet the word pulpit is not properly translated by pointing to any architectural design or even to the thing itself, just as the Bible does not come alive when you point to a black book, however gorgeously produced. Nothing of theological significance is said by simply pointing at it. There is no point, if I may so put it, in pointing at a pulpit if one is not pointing to the God of history and the God who was in Christ. In the story of the church the pulpit at its best signifies, as Herman Melville put it, that the world's a ship on its passage out and the pulpit is the prow of the world. Those who complain about Father Mapple's symbolic separation from his congregation because of his responsibility for prophecy are blind to the rebellion of the world. 'If we obey God,' says the preacher, 'we must disobey ourselves; and it is in this disobeying ourselves, wherein the hardness of obeying God consists.' This has been a constant theme from Paul the Apostle to Bonhoeffer and Paul Schneider and will remain so as long as the church lives. No preacher can be so intimately identified with his congregation that they do not feel he represents something beyond the common run of human desires and ambitions. When that day comes the work of the church will have come to an end, as one day it will, but that day is not yet.

The modern alternatives to preaching and responsibility for the spoken word may be summed up in 'dialogue' and 'happenings'. It is sometimes supposed that by using what is assumed to be a novel name some entirely new way has been discovered. It is then necessary to compare the best of the new thing with the worst of the old in order to justify the claim. Thus in the activity of dialogue, an intelligent sharing by this modern 'communicator' with other people and a sympathetic ear to their views is contrasted with some earlier preacher garrisoned in a pulpit offering a stream of platitudes and clichés to a bored congregation. Having set up the argument in this way the conclusion is reached that no one listens to this traditional preacher any more. None should be surprised at this. Indeed if this were a true description of traditional preaching the astonishing thing would be that anyone had ever listened to it. Dialogue, touching, the beaming of messages are all in fashion today and we should be foolish not to recognize the value in some of these modern insights.

2

Dialogue and Happening

The way of dialogue is seen supremely in the experience of Klaus Klostermaier in Vrindaban[1]. In the place where Krishna romped with the milkmaids and fell in love with Radha, Klostermaier, a Roman Catholic monk, lived among the people in friendship and growing understanding. He found that dialogue in depth shatters the self-confidence of those who regard themselves as the sole custodians of the whole truth. He was humble enough to spend time discovering the dialect of people of another faith and sometimes the discipline in human understanding seemed like learning several languages. Missionary activity has not always been as civilized nor shown such gentle understanding. But Klostermaier is also aware that any true dialogue must be distinguished from the false by a challenge which affects all the people engaged in it. He will not be persuaded, for example, to speak of Christ as an 'avatar' simply to accommodate Hindu views of divine appearances. This dialogue in which a man engages, both within himself and with others, has a saving tone about it. It touches the heart of the Christian faith and since it can so easily be smothered by bigotry and pride it will be well to rejoice in it wherever it may be found.

Yet while respecting all this sense of Christ in the inner life we must beware of the woeful illusions it contains. If a man steeped in Christian tradition and schooled in the literature and life of another faith tries to persuade us that this is common experience then we ought to know that we are being deceived.

There are many who speak of dialogue in depth when they are being conformed to the prevailing mood of what is sometimes called 'modern consciousness'. There is in fact no dialogue at all, but merely submission. Rebelling from every known authority people frequently interpret popular emotional spasms as the movement of the Holy Spirit. The so-called depth can soon be plumbed. What looked like the ocean turns out to be a series of shallow pools illuminated by artificial light.

My illustration of dialogue, at its best, between a Roman Catholic monk and Hindus is not typical of the world in which we live. Hinduism has always displayed such an air of tolerance that it can absorb almost anything, bringing a seeming harmony out of discord. This tolerance, however, is also a weakness and it has been said with some justice that a great tragedy with the religions of India is that they were never able to say 'No'. Dialogue, as a suggested alternative to the sermon, cannot be confined to those who are prepared for diligent study of a vast body of religious literature. If it were we might confidently prophesy that religion in general and Christianity in particular would disappear, as a force in the lives of men, more swiftly than even the gloomiest pessimists predict. We must not even allow ourselves to be restricted to the absurd views about the capacity of a university elite to spin new and abiding values, spider-like, from their own insides. The best that 'dialogue' can achieve is the sharing, rebuke and encouragement which may be found in a community of people who are open to each other. This will depend on the quality of life and the depth of experience of the people who make up the group. It is a way of life which has some link with the Hebrew view of truth where there is always a sense of relationship and covenant rather than an eternal fixed state, an abiding certainty.

The sponsors of dialogue go far beyond this. Anxious to preserve the truth that the word, incarnate in Christ, is in all of us they are prone to neglect the traditional theology of the word altogether. Since we have the equipment for rearranging the good life within us Jesus becomes a pattern who can be produced from time to time to confirm or deny our intuitions. Jesus, along with other Bible characters, on this understanding will produce more confusion than already exists in the teaching of the church. We have seen signs of this already. It is the habit of all of us to construct a theology which suits our needs but the Bible and tradition offer some safeguards. Where there is a point of reference which enshrines the heart of the faith even the teaching of the Dutch Reformed Church on race may be open to change and reform. If the interpretation of the church theologians relies solely on the opinions of the white minority in terms of their hopes and fears there will be no yielding of the iron laws. Yet people who see this have a difficulty in realizing that when their own home-spun beliefs are regarded as normative it is the pressure of the world in which they live which is likely to prevail. There is in consequence an obsession with causes currently regarded as all important.

There lies to hand a period of church history in Britain which can well serve as both an encouragement and a warning in any talk of 'modern consciousness'. Towards the end of the last century traditional views of Christianity and the Bible were causing some concern. The storm broke over Darwin's *Origin of Species*, the volume of essays called, *Essays and Reviews* and the mathematical doubts of Bishop Colenso over the arithmetical weaknesses of the Pentateuch. In the effort to understand what was happening, the church was steadied by the thought of people like F. D. Maurice, McLeod Campbell and Thomas Erskine of Linlathen. Erskine, in the shadows, brought a great light to a bewildered people and F. D. Maurice, who came out of the shade, owed him an enormous debt. Erskine, like Coleridge, was an apostle of what was called 'Christian consciousness'. This was the theme of his first book, *The Internal Evidence*, and the whole range of his argument is not to deny external authority but to show that it can have no significance apart from the response of man. 'Experience' in his teaching is not something to be set against the authority of Bible and church because a religious experience is mediated through them. In both Bible and church the important factor is the religious consciousness of men in a fellowship. Hence both Erskine and Maurice spoke of Christ within every man and his divine headship of humanity. They were concerned about 'Christian consciousness' and spoke of this rather than 'modern consciousness' because they were well aware that though we may speak of Christ in every man there are also many other things in man. Moreover, they did not make the mistake of assuming themselves to be infallible because they believed they had a key to the universe. The Bible was always to hand reminding them of true humility.

The 'Christian consciousness' of Erskine and Maurice had a further merit. It did not make the mistake of omitting proclamation of the gospel; in fact it became the more essential. Although there was a strong revolt against contemporary preaching there was also a recognition of the source of this Christ within – 'Christ in you, the hope of glory'. This must be proclaimed. 'Modern consciousness' follows a very different line. It is suspicious of all proclamation. Being intent on listening to what people say it is left without anything to say to the people. The pulpit in the prow has given way to dialogue in the stern.

There are some who, while willing to recognize the power of great orators, view the common priest and preacher as pathetic potterers. They were people without native skill or academic gifts. If this is true then their combined achievements, in human terms, must be one of the rare miracles of history. Herbert Butterfield notes how readily his fellow historians, seeking to fix their eyes on significant events, fail to see what is under their nose:

> The ordinary historian, when he comes, shall we say, to the year 1800 does not think to point out to his readers that in this year, still, as in so many previous years, thousands and thousands of priests and ministers were preaching the Gospel week in and week out, constantly reminding the farmer and the shopkeeper of charity and humility, persuading them to think for a moment about the great issues of life, and inducing them to confess their sins. Yet this was a phenomenon calculated greatly to alter the quality of life and the very texture of human history; and it has been the standing work of the Church throughout the ages – even under the worst of popes here was a light that never went out.[2]

When I consider this I find it impossible to believe that the day of proclamation has ended. It sometimes seems that it has only just begun.

The resistance to the sermon is expressed in another way. It seems that people become aware that dialogue does not adequately describe their experiences and so they also speak of 'happenings'. Preaching, it is said, is being rejected as a habit and affirmed as a happening. A happening, therefore, is occasional. It cannot submit to the burden of consistency. It comes in fits and starts and these are interpreted in the language of experience. Often it appears to be a spiritual orgasm. It is therefore measured by feeling and in no way by duty. The thought that worship is 'incumbent upon man', as Wheeler Robinson used to put it, sounds like a foreign tongue. The orgasm may be induced by changing forms and postures and by responding freely to the occasion. In this way there is excitement, stimulation and a sense that the thongs which hold traditional worshippers in thrall have been broken. The received forms, both the inner content and the outward shape, are shattered. You put the cat out at night and open the door to a tiger in the morning. Frequently the exercise is celebrated in the presence of a self-effacing chaplain who would not be so vulgar as to indulge in proclamation. He presides but does not interfere, allowing things to take their course – to happen – according to the prevailing mood. He is, by nature and calling, in the tradition of the 'baalim' finding nature worship more acceptable than the tiresome ways of the God of history.

The 'happening'[3] is often associated with drama either in a church building or elsewhere. It claims to confront and assault the audience forcing it to change and modify a view which has been held too comfortably. In mood it appears to be a blood relation of aggressive evangelism which demands an immediate decision. In form and appearance it is quite different although it both compels the will and violates the mind. As with 'dialogue', which sometimes is blatantly different from the traditional theology of the word, so it is obvious that the 'happening' enjoys a similar rebellion. Indeed we may assume that it will always be so where the feeling and response of the worshipper is given priority over any sense of the wonder and holiness of God. Where the emphasis is on the feelings people get on such an occasion there is a strong temptation to use any method which may stimulate and excite. The early spontaneity reveals tricks which work and these are then used in a more studied way to produce the desired effect. There are perils here similar to the ease with which proclamation may descend into propaganda. Both, deliberately or unwittingly, manipulate the people and this is an end which must be viewed with grave suspicion.

Happenings similar to those we have been considering are most likely in a society which is hospitable to any kind of god or which cherishes 'religious feelings' without having an acknowledged God at all. Hinduism, especially in Western Radha-Krishna dress, invites more exciting possibilities than the God of Abraham, Isaac and Jacob. I suspect that a happening was more likely while Aaron was in charge than when Moses came down from the mount with the tablets of the Law in his hands. Prancing around the golden calf which had seemed such a delightful celebration soon came to an end under the eye of Moses. Liberty in the Spirit must always be linked with obedience and the rough way of a jealous God. People may fool themselves that they can dance into the promised land without being bothered about the God who sets men free – and perhaps they could were it not for the vast, monotonous wilderness of sand that lies in between. It is, therefore, possible that the notion of the 'death of God', which has so many subtle interpretations attached to it, has encouraged people generally to exult in a religion which stimulates the sense without any demanding word. The prophets, it is true, sometimes performed strange mimes both to picture and to bring to effect their messages. But it is also clear that they were not merely responding to any passing sensation. That was a mark of a false prophet. The true prophet knew that he was bound to the word: 'Thus saith the Lord', whether he liked it or not.

Despite these strictures on 'happenings' we must recognize that they cannot be summarily dismissed. This will be the temptation of those who are bound by tradition. These, having elevated an institution to absurd heights, will be inclined to view any change as heretical. I think this is the reason for the neurotic way in which people sometimes feel forced to rebel against an authority which they have only recently learned to question. Jesus is pictured as a rebel, a hippie, a superstar –

anything in fact which appears idiosyncratic to the traditionalist but which is nevertheless stubbornly conformist. It is difficult to revolt against some immovable institution without appearing to have invented the Christian faith oneself. You have to scream in order to be heard at all. Similarly, absurd claims for the Bible have made people react in attitudes which suggest that they do not value the Bible in any way. With this newly-discovered freedom and the possibility of revolt, the word – in the sense of preaching – and the sacraments are the obvious targets. After all these are the essential marks of the church and if you become impatient with the church then you suspect the marks of the church too. This is done quite simply – the sermon becomes an occasional thing of fancy distinguished by novelty and brevity and the sacraments dissolve into theatre.

We must, however, allow for extravagance in any movement of the Spirit although, of course, we have it on good authority that there are spirits of different kinds. It is not easy to distinguish or control the forces that move people from time to time. Those who want to keep everything tidy and under proper control – by which they usually mean their own – have little understanding of the nature of enthusiasm. Throughout the story of Israel and the Christian church there are experiences which ought to help us to understand the conflict between the bursts of new life and the iron hand of authority. They also tell us something about the relationship between them. In the complicated story of the beginning of prophecy in the Old Testament there was a tendency to emphasize the ecstasy of the prophet as the distinguishing feature. So much so that ecstasy was, frequently, deliberately induced. But gradually the 'abnormal experience' was driven to the circumference and emphasis was laid on the moral content of the message. Although we may not always be able to distinguish between what is true and false in a prophetic word, we have a pretty good idea. No one is able to make the decision for us and the authority, though slender, is, at least, as reliable as the optic nerve.

The significant thing for us is not so much the beginning as the alleged end of prophecy. After the time of Ezra the Jews had a vague idea that the age of prophecy had come to an end and that the age of tradition had begun. In the age of the Maccabeans the prophets were believed to be no more. When the prophetic river had become a stream, the stream in time running dry, revelation was sought elsewhere. All revelation, so runs the creed of orthodox Judaism, is contained in the Torah. Unlike prophetic inspiration this is an unfailing source comprising all wisdom and all possible revelation. The Day of Pentecost was normally marked by the celebration of the giving of the Law at Sinai. It is little wonder that Luke hardly knew how to describe this new Pentecost. The system of the Law was shattered and the people were entering a new age because they were open to the Spirit's power. It needed an avalanche to rip away the institutions grounded on inhuman complacency. On that day, so the story in Acts says, there was taste of an intoxicating wine of a new freedom and the onlookers witnessed an exuberance which alarmed them as though nature itself brought a threat to established things.

It would be well to notice that in the story of Pentecost there was not only the ecstasy born of the Holy Spirit but also feelings and visions put into words. It was, of course, a long time ago but Peter at least felt that the occasion called for a sermon. The point is that a new language was born and it gave some sense and shape to the jumble of gestures and ecstatic cries. It seems that they sensed the way forward out of the cruel security in which they had been imprisoned. The Holy Spirit for all the excitement he brought had been baptized into the death of Christ and Calvary had become the gateway to Pentecost. This was the significance of the 'sermon' and without the interpretation it gave the early zeal might well have been nothing but froth. It is also significant that Paul goes to some pains to tell the churches about the difference between inspiration and insanity. It is as though we reach the full flow of the river, having seen the waters near the source bubble and foam. The fruits of the Spirit, says Paul, are love, joy, peace, patience, kindness, goodness, faithfulness, gentleness and self-control (Gal. 5. 22, 23). That is not a bad list to measure a 'happening' or, for that matter, an institution that glories in its tradition. No one who takes the gift of the Holy Spirit seriously can ignore the ecstasy which was created, the giving of the Law which was fulfilled in Christ nor the significance of the proclaimed gospel. All these find an abiding place in the church and its mission. It is a three-fold cord that cannot easily be broken.

One of the fears of those who favour 'happenings' over against the preaching of the word is the danger of the preacher being isolated, having no human link with the people. We shall have more to say about this and for the moment it may be accepted as a salutary warning . . . It is easy for a preacher to be detached and in these days his own insecurity in a growingly professional society may well make him more removed and pompous than he would otherwise be. If the least envy of the position of others invades his heart he is already on a perilous path. It is true that a vocation which had advantages of education has now lost them. It is true that the preacher cannot any longer claim to be more knowledgeable than his people on a whole variety of subjects. It is true that even in the disciplines which are supposed to be a part of his calling he cannot be over-confident in speaking about them. Yet none of these touch the heart of the matter and none should hinder the authority of an experience which is rooted in the faith. Pascal knew long ago that it was not the God of the philosophers who had brought the fire. More recent writers have lamented the sway of 'cerebral' religion, especially in Protestantism. Since this intellectual obsession has so limited the nature of Christian experience there is little point in lamenting its demise – even in the clergy.

Yet I think that in the past the preacher and the people have shown a remarkable fellowship in a common ministry. My own experience, at least, is of men who shared the lives of the people with care and understanding. It was not uncommon for a minister to know his people – their names and characters, strength and weakness – and to share intimately in their joys and sorrows. He celebrated each significant occasion in their lives and they turned to him at times when they would have turned to no other. Perhaps those days have gone but there is little point in clouding memories of the past in order to make the present seem clear. We must look more carefully at this minister of the word and sacraments before we dig his grave.

3

The Popular Preacher

The ministry of the word is generally understood in terms of preaching. Although this emphasis is, by itself, a limitation on its full meaning there can be no doubt that the sermon has always been an essential part of the ministry of the church. Moreover, this is true not only of evangelism and missionary activity but of the ministry of the church to itself. It was like the breaking of bread in the sacrament and people learned to take refuge in the preached word as in the blood of Christ. By it their life was nourished and what began in conversion was sustained and enriched in the continuing Christian Way.

Although in the early centuries of the Christian church there were few outstanding preachers, it is not hard to see how the popular preacher made his appearance. Since some were able to speak more effectively and persuasively than others the crowds came to hear them and the pedigree reaches back, at least, to Chrysostom in the East and Augustine in the West. In the story of *The City Temple 1640–1940*[1] Leslie Weatherhead, who was minister at the time, contributed a Foreword in which he deals with the problem of the popular preacher. It is a problem because the path to popularity is one of devious temptations. Weatherhead knew better than most the envy of some of his fellow ministers because they struggled to do what he did so well. The Foreword is marked by unusual aggression and it is not difficult to sense his own battle with resentment. Yet he has little difficulty in showing that although the word popular, in this context, is an ambiguous one he is not ashamed to be interesting even if others delight in being dull. Weatherhead ends by saying, 'For I regard preaching as the highest of all the arts, and the work of trying to convey all that Christ can be to the human heart, the greatest privilege which life offers.' In what sense then may one speak of preaching as an art?

It is quite obvious that the moment a man takes it upon himself to speak to others his performance will be judged in ways which may please or offend. He may, of course, claim to be unmoved by either. A political speaker may well be delighted if he gains the disapproval of his hearers. If he considers himself a prophet it would be bordering on insult to agree too readily with all that he says. If, on the other hand, he is anxious that his gifts should be used for the benefit of a constituency, we may suppose that he hopes his election address, at least, will be received with some favour. It would seem a little pointless to welcome wholesale opposition on such an occasion. It is possible that in sponsoring views which are not popular he expects disagreement. Yet even then, as one desiring to persuade, he will hope to gain converts. He knows, too, that if he is to 'communicate' it will be wise to have both a programme to offer and some skill in presenting it. In time he will discover that it matters a good deal whether people agree or not. He will be secretly pleased when people compliment him on his speech and happy that someone has referred kindly to his television image. Depending on his party and temperament he will be encouraged by hearing that he is another Lloyd George, Churchill or Aneurin Bevan or that his unassuming manner has made someone recall Rab Butler. Whatever strange emotions may invade him we can be quite sure that he will be pleased to 'communicate' even though the message has been considerably warped in the process. This, indeed, is often a distinct advantage. Political speeches and dialogues vary from age to age but always at their best there is some semblance of political art in the presentation.

A popular preacher or almost any public speaker is in a similar position. The preacher, however, has additional complications. He cannot enjoy even innocent pleasure in his image because he spends a good deal of time, if he is faithful to his calling, telling people that his image is of no significance. The people who come are to see Christ, not the preacher. An ambitious politician may also claim that he is pointing to a cause or to the party and not to himself. Few people believe him, however, because they know that if he has any ambition and some gifts he wants to be the leader. The more frequently he denies this the more people see through the image. Ambition, while proper in a politician, is not seemly in a parson. Archbishop Lang said of his portrait by Sir William Orpen: 'They say in that portrait I look proud, prelatical and pompous.' He made the remark in the hearing of Dr Hensley Henson who is reputed to have replied, 'And may I ask Your Grace to which of these epithets Your Grace takes exception?' I suspect that this exchange was not just to Archbishop Lang but it is certainly worth remembering that while ambition, display and a hunger for success may be commendable in a politician, with a preacher it is not so. He will fare best by recalling the response of Massillon who said when he was congratulated on his preaching, 'The devil has already told me this more eloquently than you.' I am not claiming that this distinction between politician and preacher is fixed or entirely visible. Indeed it is not so, but the corruption of the preacher who desires his own success is sure though not always swift. In terms of worldly repute he is at a distinct disadvantage because he claims to represent already a new creation which is not of his devising. Similarly, originality and arguments are not available to enhance the prestige of the preacher. How can he be original about something he has received or boast when he knows that he can but accept all that comes to him as a gift? And if he is tempted to be proud of the logic and sweep of his argument he would do well to ponder Thomas Erskine's question when he heard that a preacher had produced some good arguments: 'Arguments about what?'

You will observe that the preacher finds himself in a strange predicament. Having gifts, he is not meant to display them; engaged in the art of public speaking, he must dispense with compliments. Since he cannot be humble by will-power he falls easily into a parsonic caricature. Here, of course, we are touching the heart of what the Christian life means. If the life of a

Christian is hid with Christ in God the preacher, however popular, cannot be the exception. No man dare preach with his gifts although it may be supposed that this is not a great danger for many. Truth through personality may be permissible for a saint but for most preachers it is an open invitation to self-display. The possibility of a man with gifts preaching as though he were not aware of them depends upon the truth of the Christian way itself. It will be the mark of a man in Christ. That oratory and rhetoric are not in themselves enough, in any age, is obvious. A preacher may display all the gifts of public speech and yet fail to kindle a spark of true religion. I had ample opportunity to learn this in my youth. Born in the waning light of the Welsh revival, I saw preachers frantically trying to recover what they considered to be a genuine experience of the Holy Spirit in their own young days. This means that in my own boyhood I heard much talk of preaching gifts, enjoyable meetings and good times where men who knew about the dying revival tried to work up a fervour as they flogged an old story. There were preachers, noted for their entertaining gifts, who played with words and indulged in the Welsh love of alliteration. The circus of big meetings was their meat and drink and, being skilled in the art of communication, they were tempted to feel that having offered a series of pulpit platitudes in a pleasing way their work was done. They were the forerunners of the evangelical promoters.

Yet if public speaking is in any way an art a preacher cannot avoid its perils without pretending that it matters little how a man speaks. Since it matters much it may be helpful to look at forms of this art and, by doing so, some oblique shafts of light may fall on the act of preaching. I propose, therefore, to consider three different ways in which we may use the word art to describe the relationship between a speaker and the audience. A congregation should never merely be understood in terms of people who listen as though they were entirely separate from the preacher. This is why it is better to speak of a congregation rather than an audience. But I am concerned primarily, at present, with the relationship between one person and others in terms of address and communication. The three forms are – high art, pop art and mass art.

There is a sense in which high art is not aware of the audience. The artist, wrestling with his own experience, is not over-anxious about the impression he is creating. He does not cut and trim with a view to applause. Sometimes he is forced to consider himself and his family but his one passion is to give what he has felt and seen. Popularity is neither his aim nor his craft. Indeed there are times when he seems to covet the mysterious and obscure as though he felt that familiar things encouraged only a surface view of what is essentially profound. Or, better still, he may take what is familiar, like Van Gogh gazing at a field of corn, and reveal things which previously were hidden. This is the art which enlarges the experience of others. They are taken beyond their own experiences by the vision of the artist. There is nothing calculated about this for the artist writes or paints and those who are willing to be open to his view are both challenged and disturbed. There is also in art of this quality a testament of beauty which brings a new creative power into our understanding of life.

It may well seem a daunting task to discover art of this nature in the forbidding folios of the old divines. They have been neglected sadly because they were often engaged in controversies in which we have long lost interest. The sermons of the fathers of the church are no longer read but when someone distils their wisdom and power in selections from this great mass of literature we know we are near to a source of inspiration. John Donne from the seventeenth century is perhaps the outstanding example. Much in his many sermons is not attractive to us. Indeed it is distasteful, with its concentration on old divinity. Yet his wisdom and experience, his rich imagination, pour out and all this is made the more impressive by the solemnity of the scene and the congregation eager to listen. Donne, moreover, was aware of the importance of style and language. In one of his sermons he speaks of the preacher, in musical terms, as the trumpet's voice, the bell of warning, 'a lovely song, sung to an instrument' . . . his style should be as the style of the Holy Ghost, 'a diligent, and an artificial style'. So he speaks of melody, harmony and delight. It is clear that the word on sin and death and God could not be offered in a casual way with the preacher leaning nonchalantly on the pulpit. The art was disciplined and purified by the glory of the word.

Style and language may enthral a congregation but I think that the touch of high art within a sermon needs also a prophetic quality. Here the language may not be beautiful but it gains in power because the message is urgent. Frequently it goes beyond the hearers and is not content to feed on what people want or what they may feel they have a right to demand because they pay the preacher. True prophecy is always bound to the word of God in the Bible and in the tradition of the church. It is not limited to any narrow interpretation, for there is liberty in the word. Yet it does not strive to be prophetic by indulging in novelty and passing fancies. A man may sometimes deceive both his hearers and himself by rhetoric which could just as easily appear in a weekly newspaper during a Party Conference. Although he dignifies it by a text, hastily pushed in at the top, time will soon tell that he is exercising in propaganda and not engaged in prophecy. Prophecy is spoken to the times, but it belongs to the ages.

There should be some element of high art in every preacher, however artless he appears. He has a source beyond his own resources and the well is deep. When the preacher wrestles with his own experiences there is a bridge between the present and the past. People today who favour happenings rather than traditional worship have sometimes recorded their sense of gratitude to someone who has spoken out of his own struggling experience. The sense of a communication which is not complete, not polished and finished in any dogmatic way, has a strong attraction in an age when the people themselves are seeking and struggling. There is one experience which I shall always remember which confirms, for me, this kind of impact. I went one Sunday during my summer holiday to a little chapel in Cardiganshire where the service was in the Welsh language. The congregation was small, made up of people from the farms near by. The preacher was thin and pale with dark, blue marks of coaldust deep in his face from the days when he had been a miner. His language was lovely like the tongue of a bard and his theme was resurrection. He told us that to believe in resurrection was a wonderful thing for the fulfilment of life not yet made complete . . . for a nation struggling hopefully towards the promised land . . . And then he paused and went on quietly to tell us that there were times when a dry doubt came over him and he could not say whether he believed or not. At the close of the service I heard that the preacher, but a little time before, had lost in this changing life his only daughter. The blow had been swift and grievous. It was this struggle with doubt which impressed so much and made it impossible to forget.

There are, however, two warning signs of which we should take some notice. Unlike most warning signs they are not prohibitions but gentle reminders that even the most attractive ways may be fraught with danger. The first is that if the preacher dwells for too many Sundays in the realms of high art he will soon find that his congregation is sadly diminished. While the preacher is walking high he will have lost any link with his people and they will be floundering in some miserable mud-pit of which he was blissfully unaware. The second warning comes, strangely as some will think, from Rudolf Bultmann. He asks questions about the nature of art in this context. Is it expressing anything but man himself in his rich and abysmal possibilities? He admits that art may serve a real purpose by laying bare human existence in its depth. He then puts a further solemn question: 'But is it therefore God speaking, or only man, probing to the ground of his being, speaking to himself?'[2]

Pop art is different from 'high art' but the distinction is not as clear as some would imagine. In relation to preaching it may be difficult to see any relevance at all. People accustomed to swift judgments on subjects about which they are ignorant will be tempted to dismiss pop art out of hand because they associate it with something they regard as unpleasant. So let me coax the stubborn and any who may reject pop art on some unspecified grounds of sophistication. T. S. Eliot, in *Selected Essays*, pays a remarkable tribute to Marie Lloyd. The association seems unnatural and this in itself should give cause for reflection. Eliot writes:

> Whereas other comedians amuse their audiences as much and sometimes more than Marie Lloyd, no other comedian succeeded so well in giving expression to the life of that

> audience, in raising it to a kind of art. It was, I think, this capacity for expressing the soul of the people that made Marie Lloyd unique, and that made her audiences, even when they joined in the chorus, not so much hilarious as happy.[3]

The pop artist is given to confirming, to reassuring his audience. He does not challenge or disturb although the laughter is often mingled with tears. As with jazz he is always creating something new from music that seems essentially the same. He feels the audience in his bones, responding to them and they to him, so that distance (six feet above contradiction!) is eclipsed. Aware of his audience, he is not in subjection to it. The artist and the audience depend on each other.

It may seem strange to mention Paul Tillich in this company, but, on his own confession, it was his habit to approach a pulpit with fear and trembling. Yet he says that his relationship with the 'audience' gave him a pervasive sense of joy, the joy of creative communion, of giving and taking. This experience is, I believe, the nearest approach to popular preaching in artistic terms. Older readers who feel that Tillich went the wrong way may be comforted to know that H. R. Mackintosh was described as a popular preacher for similar reasons.

I have already referred to the temptations which I witnessed in my childhood of this way where there was a love of word-play and, sometimes, cheap entertainment. Yet there was good in it too. The preacher had a close relationship with his congregation and this was made the easier by the 'big-seat', where the deacons sat, so that he was able to speak conversationally to them while the people shared the intimacy. The chapels were admirably constructed for this purpose and most of them encouraged a feeling of friendship. Since the pulpit was near to the people, on the floor and in the gallery, every gesture, smile or grimace carried its message. Laughter and comfort, fear and trembling and every varying mood were swiftly passed from one person to another. Once or twice I remember hearing the 'hwyl' when speech poured out like a song and, in full sail, the words took wings as they were borne by the wind of the Spirit. The preacher no longer manipulated the text, the words controlled him. The popular synthetic dispensers of the 'hwyl' seemed to be able to produce it when they pleased simply by a sudden switch in the pitch of the voice. But the scene I now recall is the sublime conversation of the preacher with his congregation, especially with the deacons, and their spoken response as they were encouraged, rebuked and confirmed in the faith. It was pop art in the chapel while the preacher entertained as surely as he inspired the people.

Mass art is of a different nature from high and pop art. We can identify the people who are truly enriched by the creative artist. The pop audience is also not difficult to find and the people in it enjoy being together feeling the strong link with the artist. Masses, however, are difficult to locate. To speak of the mass of the people is to reveal a way of looking at others. It says nothing about the people themselves because in a sad sense they have ceased to be viewed as people. Mass art, since it shares some of the features of pop art, is not wholly evil though it is ever in danger of becoming so. At the worst it is the art of the demagogue who seeks to manipulate the people and can do so only by lumping them together in a mass so that their value as persons ceases to be. The instrument here, which enables control to be realized, is propaganda, which is spread over the land like manure or belched out of microphones according to the means of communication which may be favoured. Even the word communication, which is not a pleasing one, is debased when used in this way.

It is perhaps unfair to describe Liberace simply as a mass artist though he has set out the method better than anyone else. 'My whole trick', he says, 'is to keep the tune well out in front. If I play Tchaikovsky I play his melodies and skip his spiritual struggles. Naturally I condense. I have to know just how many notes my audience will stand for. If there's time left over I fill in with a lot of runs up and down the keyboard.'[4] I think that Liberace has some of the features of pop art but here he reveals a man nervously aware of his audience and fearful lest he should lose touch. It is clear that, despite the smile, he is doing things to the audience rather than experiencing a sense of joy at being one with it.

When popular preaching becomes mass art the fate of

hearers and performers is sealed. There is fortunately a way of escape in that the mass audience usually does not endure. Under a dictatorship, however, the mass approach to people remains. People are treated in this way in their homes, at work and at play as well as when they are gathered together in frightful festivals. The mass audience at a religious meeting disperses and it is possible for some of the people in their homes to regain sanity. They are not constantly subjected to mass propaganda. But alas! Professional promoters of mass enterprises in religion practise enough of the tricks of the trade to put us on guard. If a crowd gathers then it must be retained for the season at all costs. We may recall Billy Graham lying awake, night after night, wondering whether the hall in which a campaign was to be held would be full. His wife also suffered from a similar disturbance in her mind but for her it came as a dream turning into a nightmare of empty seats. Charity compels me to suggest that humility may have been a cause of this anxiety. Yet if most preachers in Britain were similarly afflicted they would all long ago have perished from nervous exhaustion. Concern that people should hear the Word is good but our Lord did not favour the way of the over-anxious. It is worth noting that when Jesus saw a crowd – let alone a mass – he not only had compassion on them but also dispersed them and went away to some quiet place for a while.

There are, then, features of art at different levels which tell us something about the work of the preacher. It is perhaps more needful to beware of the dangers of a self-conscious art than of the virtues in high art. Preachers who have popular appeal need to remember the temptation to fill in time with a lot of runs up and down the keyboard as they skip the spiritual struggles.

4

Truth through Personality?

Although I have spent some time in the previous chapter discussing some ways in which a sermon and the act of preaching may be viewed as an art, I have few illusions about this way. The emphasis on the art may arise from a love of fine speech and telling gesture. It may be a reaction from what is constrained and unnatural or what is uncouth and vulgar. Style in speech and gesture vary a great deal but there are times when incompetence is the very thing which spoils the effectiveness of what a man is saying. It is interesting to look again at the remarkable series of lectures[1] which C. H. Spurgeon gave to his students. He himself was an artist in both the written and spoken word and he wanted his students to be well-equipped for their work. For this reason he gives a lot of space to the voice, to postures, action and gesture. The lectures have justly become classics but that may be one of the reasons why they are not widely read today. Abounding in humanity, Spurgeon had wit and humour uncommon in the preachers of his day or any day. Where Spurgeon is dealing with pretension and humbug he produces comic writing which is almost beyond compare. Yet he knew well that these excursions into the art of speaking are not the most important thing, though they are not as trivial as the solemn may suppose. Spurgeon knew that if a preacher is talking of heaven or hell it is wise to point in the right direction.

In many centuries there has been little doubt about the truth of the Christian message. This does not mean that it has been accepted by all but that those who professed it believed that in the Bible and their articles of faith there were infallible truths in which they could trust. It was not common for people to consider the Bible to be vulnerable. Moreover, people in the Western world outside the church were not marked by much sophistication in offering agnostic or atheistic views. Until modern times these exercises were performed by a comparatively small number of individual persons. Widespread unbelief in this sense was not found among the people and although they might not be open in professing the Christian faith, they had the feeling they should. Preaching in an age of concealed belief is very different from the intellectual revolt which we have witnessed. If you feel that sin and ignorance have to be overcome, then to seek ways to convict and persuade are of cardinal importance. Our age is marked by the preacher being perplexed more about what he has to say than how he is to say it. His trouble is not what he should do with his arms and legs or how he should use his voice but whether there is anything distinctive to say at all.

This change, though spread over many years, has finally struck home with dramatic intensity. Yet before we consider the nature of the message we must spend some time understanding what has taken place. When John Wesley advised the preacher never to clap his hands or thump the pulpit he was dealing with what he considered to be an extravagance which would have a bad effect on offering the gospel. But despite his own struggles over faith he had no doubt that there was a gospel to offer and that he could train converted people to give it. It was the same with Spurgeon and, of course, many others. It must also be remembered that Nonconformity had to give special attention to training for the ministry because many of the students had no prospect of adult education other than what was provided at the dissenting academies. There were a number of recognized textbooks which, under the direction of tutors, gave to these students a systematic theological training. In addition there was some apologetics but in the main the colleges had a fixed course which endured through many years and which was believed to deal with the substance of the gospel. Since many of the young men who responded to a call to the ministry had no background of education, homiletics was prominently featured in the course. Included in this were lectures on preaching and the best way of presenting the Christian faith to the world. Early modern books on preaching spend a good deal of time on style, illustrations, structure, reading, the writing of sermons and similar themes. It was necessary to introduce the students to the preparation and delivery of sermons and to give at the same time, guidance in reading and study.

When I recall the homiletics I received at college I am surprised to notice how much time was given to craft and art. The result of all this was that, inevitably, we thought of the sermon as an art form and the act of preaching, in Phillips Brooks' phrase, as 'truth through personality'. It is perhaps unfair to load my teachers and Phillips Brooks with the grievous responsibility for all the ills that came from this emphasis. Yet it seems clear now that on this understanding ministers become divided into those who can preach and those who can't. Preaching, like singing or writing poetry, was regarded as a native gift. Some men had the gift because they could project their personalities and had attractive and winning ways. There were others who by pushing and prodding were made capable of producing some kind of tune even though it were restricted to the black notes. During my college course, with all these lectures on the art of preaching, Douglas Stewart, later the Assistant Head of Religious Broadcasting with the BBC, arrived and without ceremony began an attack on the cult of preaching as truth through personality.[2] It was a rough exposure of the way in which the students thought they could preach by making a sermon like building a house or constructing a table and selling it with the flair of a commercial traveller.

I am quite sure that this warning was a salutary one. It is possible to listen to what are regarded as well-constructed sermons and to decide that this sort of activity is best left to a few. A preacher may even excuse his lack of ability in this direction by implying that he has other gifts instead. I belong to a tradition where all who respond to the call to the ministry are expected to preach. It serves no purpose when a man is a minister of the sacraments only – the word and sacraments are bound indissolubly together. Living sermons grow like plants. They are not constructed like tables. It is confusion about this attitude which compels preachers to wonder how they can possibly sustain such a ministry. Those who think that a sermon may be produced once a month or at some other decent regular interval are still held by the idea of building operations rather than the word which the Spirit gives. When a preacher is aware of the gospel he is called to offer and sensitive to the needs of people the burden of sermon preparation will be lifted as by a miracle.

It is the dilemma of the modern preacher and the bewilderment of the people with which we are concerned now. I said at the beginning of this chapter that it was the lack of a message rather than the method of delivery which had produced a crisis in the ministry. I find this illustrated in a lecture by Thomas Jones to the Cardiff Cymmrodorrion Society in 1942. The author and the place are significant. Thomas Jones, having left Wales for London when he was seventeen years of age, had spent his time among the statesmen and political movements of his day. Closely associated with Lloyd George, he observed with a keen eye and at first hand all the great movements and troubles in European history during and for many years after the 1914–18 war. He wrote a great deal about these events and since his death there has been a series of his diaries published on these exalted themes. Having lived for so many years at the heart of world politics he returned to Wales and in *The Native Never Returns*[3] he tells something of his impressions and the changes he detected from the days of his boyhood. The country, Wales, is significant because few places had so strong a faith in the power of preaching, and the decline of the church particularly in the industrial areas has nowhere been more rapid. It would be folly to interpret this as cause and effect because the withering of the influence of the Christian way had many complicated sources.

However, Thomas Jones reports his own impressions and does so mindful of the enormous struggle in Europe. For him, behind the scenes he had witnessed for so long, there was a raging war between two absolute conceptions of the nature of man and the world. Yet in the setting of a war which affected everyone in Britain he sensed the entire absence of a note of conviction in modern preaching, where the trumpet gives forth an uncertain sound.

> I have usually heard a sermon every Sunday since my return to Wales. Of the scores of sermons I have listened to I should say not half a dozen have given me any sense of an urgent message for the congregation; that it mattered profoundly whether the preacher delivered it or not; that there was anything more than that it was to be deplored that nations were at war and that it was hoped God would bring peace soon to a stricken world. Most of the sermons are essays, lectures, talks, sometimes with a pleasant literary flavour.[4]

Thomas Jones notes that his impressions are confirmed by the views of others more thoroughly immersed in the Welsh scene – that it is not so much a fierce atheism as a crippling indifference which is the trouble, where people are not disturbed by the situation in any way.

It is, I believe, particularly helpful that Thomas Jones also described the changed attitude to Christian doctrine. In 1913 Dr Miall Edwards,[5] speaking at a Summer School of Social Service, had talked of the bearing of Christian doctrine on the solution of social problems. In doing so Edwards had viewed the trinity as the culminating point in the Christian doctrine of God, the highest and boldest reach of theological speculation, enshrining an imperishable truth. He also stressed the social significance of the doctrine of immortality. Yet in 1937 it was argued in a Welsh periodical that neither the doctrine of the trinity nor of immortality had any vital significance for a follower of Jesus Christ. Having reviewed his impressions in this way Thomas Jones adds this comment: 'What is significant is not only that opinion has radically changed, but that the public, in the churches and outside, are indifferent to the change.'

Now it would be possible to illustrate this change in many ways and in various parts of Britain. What Thomas Jones said about Wales in 1942 has become more marked in the following years. We are dealing with something much more radical than failure to put the message in an attractive form. We are in fact confronted by the question of truth itself. The point was made quite brutally in a recent university debate on belief in God. The impression rather than the details or the result of the debate remains with me. Belief was presented with skill by the Archbishop of Canterbury and the ubiquitous Malcolm Muggeridge. Many people spoke, among them Professor Alasdair MacIntyre, who has struggled manfully with difficulties of belief. His words, as I remember them, cut into the neat knots, tied by the believers, like a knife. The question, he said, was one of truth or falsehood and he made it clear that for him the claims of the believers were false.

5

What is Truth?

When I say that it is the question of truth that matters I am clearly taking a risk and heading for troubled waters. Yet to refuse to do so would be cowardly and a betrayal of the pilgrim way. It is no good either accepting or pretending to accept what we do not believe. It is equally foolish to complain that a man is preaching without conviction when he has none. Yet a man who speaks without conviction may well be striving to gain what cannot be compelled or perhaps there was a time when he did speak with conviction but somewhere along the road he has lost it. Again, the preacher may have conviction himself but be incapable of producing the kind of feelings in others which they think they ought to have. Alternatively, the congregation resting on traditional convictions may judge the preacher by their own short measuring line. The possibilities in this relationship between the preacher and the congregation seem limitless but, and of this we can be sure, the preacher must speak in terms which are recognizably related to an understanding of truth.

The difficulty we have to face is well illustrated by Alasdair MacIntyre. At the end of the last chapter I recalled his piece of surgery on the body of believers in a university debate. It was not a mere debating point because he was wanting to open up the whole question of belief. Yet in 1959 he wrote a book on *Difficulties in Christian Belief*[1] in which although recognizing the many problems he nevertheless favoured an acceptance of the mysterious ways of God. It follows from this that if the university debate had taken place about this time MacIntyre would have been found in the camp of the Archbishop. The years in between have witnessed a change in his mind. The change, as it happens, was swift. When MacIntyre wrote his book he believed in God but by the time it had reached the press he did not. In that short interval of time a remarkable and radical mental revolt had taken place. An uncharitable mind might suppose that the change was slight assuming that MacIntyre did not have much belief when he wrote about it, or that he is a man in the habit of deceiving himself. Yet, I think that the only conclusion we can reach is that here is a man of unusually keen and honest mind finding that at one moment he believes and the next he does not believe. We may assume, too, that it was not some superficial, fitful thing which worked the change but something profound and sincere.

Yet although this is the situation with Alasdair MacIntyre there would be something strange about life if this kind of search illustrated entirely what we mean by 'truth'. It is certainly an aspect of truth but there is, as MacIntyre well knows, much more to be said. If we were thinking of truth simply as an intellectual view then the vast majority of people would be left floundering while a few razor-brained pioneers marched on. Let me make the point by a quotation from MacIntyre's book assuming that his view now would be the same:

> But suppose that we could found belief in God on arguments. It is not just that our freedom would be taken away. It is also the fact that the road into the kingdom of God would be one made easier for those with a grasp of sound argument. But the qualifications for entry into the kingdom of God are after all different from those required to pass an elementary logic examination. God, if he is the God of Christian theology, speaks to shepherds and fishermen, to tax-collectors and scholars, to all sorts and conditions of men, equally and in the same way. The voice of God has to be one that all can hear; and therefore it cannot be heard by way of argument, for a capacity for argument is not common in this way.[2]

If the road into the kingdom of God is not found by argument I assume that the road out of it is not found by argument either. It would seem a shame for would-be atheists to find a lot of intellectual barriers on the way while Christians have a clear track. MacIntyre had some hidden experiences, of which I am ignorant, which prompted him to change his view. But he makes the important point that 'truth' involves more than an intellectualist view and in that, for the time being, I shall rest.

I find it interesting that this view of truth, as of the mind, appears in the most unexpected places. Martyn Lloyd-Jones in his knock-about book on *Preaching and Preachers* makes the point not once but many times. 'In preaching', he argues, 'we are to present the Truth, and, clearly, this is something first and foremost for the mind.'[3] This sentence comes in a vigorous attack on an emotional appeal for decisions. But when Martyn Lloyd-Jones talks about truth he is thinking about a 'form of teaching' or a 'form of doctrine' which had been given and which must also be preached. This particular point of view is emphasized by printing truth with a capital T, much as some distinguish the spiritual life from the activity of the 'natural' man by printing it with a capital L. So now we have an insistence on the prior importance of the mind which is not given freedom to engage in mental gymnastics but which is confronted by Truth defined in terms of Christian doctrine. This quite obviously is a limitation on what would normally be regarded as the truth. It is Truth proclaimed because it has been received already in doctrinal form and, by its nature, it makes a demand for decision. Since it is assumed that the doctrine is revealed and given by God, the mind will grasp it and understand it when it is thinking properly. To reject this Truth means that the mind is at enmity with God. The line of argument is similar to Jonathan Edwards on 'freedom of the will' and it has similar dogmatic foundations. Yet to insist in this way on the nature of truth, as 'something first and foremost for the mind', prolongs one of the problems of Protestantism in that it breeds a Christian faith which is narrowly intellectual, grimly ethical and which depends upon the hearer's mental comprehension – 'and thus inevitably a somewhat middle-class business' as John Macquarrie puts it.

It will be well to try to understand what the evangelical emphasis implies. Men who are able to accept a direct doctrinal statement of the faith, which cannot be questioned, are frequently far more impressive than their neighbouring ministers who seem to be groping blindly for some rope to which they can cling. The assurance they enjoy is communicated to their congregations who are relieved and proud to have a preacher who knows where he stands and where he is going. I suspect that the position of the evangelical is neither as sure nor abiding as we are led to believe. During most of my ministry I have walked around with evangelical daggers in my back – all planted there, let it be understood, in a Christian spirit! But I have seen some remarkable changes to which I must briefly refer. When I began my ministry I was told repeatedly by conservative ministers and laymen that the world belonged to the devil. There are, I understand, still a considerable number who hold by this view. But H. F. R. Catherwood, in a book dedicated to Martyn Lloyd-Jones,[4] goes to some pains to refute this. I am sure that his discussion about this is right on both biblical and theological grounds. It may be added that it would be a distinct disadvantage for a Christian to be Director-General of the National Economic Development Council (as Catherwood was at that time), having to explain to his colleagues that he was eager for expansion in the interests of property owned by the devil. This radical change in a conservative position is to be welcomed in the interests of truth and expediency. Again, it was fashionable for conservative Christians to insist on separation from unbelievers apart from those occasions where they could be mustered to attend an evangelical meeting. The change in this has been quite startling as may be seen in the Report of the Evangelical Alliance's Commission on Evangelism, *On the Other Side*,[5] and in the works of Francis Schaeffer.

The evangelical Christian, despite these changes, still presents a front of assurance before the world because he claims to be immovable on the fundamentals and on biblical interpretation. It is possible to alter one's view about sober dress or total abstinence without surrendering the heart of the faith, but the view of the Bible and statements about belief are in a different realm. I should not wish to foster uncertainty where confidence gives peace, but it is needful to explore how the Bible lives again and whether a brief summary of the essence of the faith is adequate for modern man. I take the view that the attempt to state in doctrinal terms 'the irreducible minimum of the faith' savours of the kind of exercise which Russell Maltby deplored. Maltby once described a Minister's Fraternal setting out to answer the question 'What is a Christian?' The Presbyterian minister began modestly by saying that he wasn't the right man for the job and Maltby says that at the end of his paper it was clear that his modesty was thoroughly justified. An Anglican then made his attempt and there was a variety of different judgments on his effort. Maltby, for his part, had always known what a Christian is but he could not get his brethren to agree with him. He then makes the comment that the mistake of the Fraternal members lay in their trying to find a minimal definition – 'to discover how many essential qualities of a sheep you can abstract from a sheep and still leave it a sheep.'

The evangelical statement for 'the irreducible minimum' goes like this: 'The first essential is belief in Jesus Christ as both fully man and fully God. The second is a realistic understanding of the plight of man as a helpless sinner before a Holy God. The third essential is belief in the atoning death and triumphant resurrection of Christ as the sole means of man's redemption from sin and reconciliation to God. The fourth essential is the response to the work of the Holy Spirit, the response of repentance and faith as a genuine turning from sin and an act of trust in God.'[6] I am not sure whether these are chronological steps or not, but the fallacy lies not in logic but in the curiously systematic way of looking at men and women. In some senses the weakness is psychological rather than doctrinal. I should have little difficulty in claiming that these essentials appear consistently in my sermons. It is therefore somewhat embarrassing to discover that when I know they are there my conservative brethren are unable to see them. I think this is because – apart from any concealed faithlessness in me – they seem to insist on the proper words coming in the right order.

There is, also, something more fundamental than this. It is

that there is a confusion between faith and correct belief. The faith which is commitment or surrender to Christ is presented too hastily and dogmatically in terms of basic beliefs which were developed over several centuries. This indecent rush at the offering of the 'full gospel' then proceeds to leave out of account the delicate, indissoluble link between history and interpretation. It looks as though it is possible to fling down naked historical facts which are picked up and absorbed, in the raw, into hungry yet perceptive minds. I do not believe that this is the way which gives abiding significance to the response of men to God and life. Indeed it leads finally to ways of enmity and division, so that if a preacher tries to present the person of Christ with a mind to his own struggles and the questions of his hearers he is summarily branded as a heretic and the hounds are let loose. The preacher, of course, may be producing a Christology which could not possibly make the dead live. But it matters little how longingly he thirsts for the truth. In the eyes of the dogmatists he has become the enemy. It has, alas, always been so where men impose systems of beliefs on others – the Orthodox have done it, the Roman Catholics for centuries, the Fascist and Marxist in modern times, and as Spurgeon once said – and he should know – the Baptists will do it if they get the chance.

I am reminded of Keri Evans (1860–1941), who gave up his University Chair in Philosophy with all the prospects of a brilliant academic career to be the minister of a little chapel in Carmarthenshire. At home with scholarship, he was also a faithful child of the Welsh Revival and a regular speaker at Keswick. Yet he writes of the growing enmity over the understanding of Christ, referring to a time, in his own life, of 'single devotion towards Christ' spoiled by the complexities of fundamentalism:

> With regard to other children of the revival, it grieves me that many of them have become entombed in the letter of the doctrine, and like 'little popes' condemn all who will not accept the kind of human system which they cherish. It appears that they are in the same state of self-assurance as Theomemphus when he was 'judging the children of his

mother, judging them sometimes justly and sometimes unjustly'. Good fruit is not proof of a good tree to them, since it is still possible to cast out devils through Beelzebub, the prince of devils![7]

I suspect that what Keri Evans claims to have observed is a true reflection of what has happened. That is, there has been a growing aggression in some preachers as they tell us confidently what the faith is and equally a growing impatience with those who feel that the very foundations have been shaken and who illustrate their doubts by all that they say. The hesitant ones seem to deny the very faith itself by their faltering advance. The reason for this conflict is clear. The church is no stranger to controversy. It has presented arguments about sacred things as a spectacle before the eyes of the world. But there has been no time comparable with ours when the searching and inquiring have been so radical. It is not simply that we can no longer hide in the decent obscurity of the Latin tongue. The whole sweep of increasing knowledge and the scientific spirit have questioned institutions and creeds which once seemed secure. It is understandable, therefore, that men under attack have responded in a number of ways. Some decide that the only sure defence is to protect what has been given. This is done by refusing to parley with the alleged enemy and to strengthen the foundations against every alien force. It is, by its nature, a strategy which refuses to take any risks. It may be seen in any institution which has a celebrated history, but more so in the church because there appear to be certain divine sanctions for an impregnable position. Men who at one time were able to live by 'a single devotion towards Christ' become wilfully aggressive because they feel that so much depends upon their ability to stand and withstand. Others simply submit to the social pressures which overwhelm any sign of resistance. They become conformist because the movement of history suggests that this is the only possible solution. Yet others seek to find a newborn faith which comes alive again, so they believe, in a new age. They do this by a considerable variety of compromises and quick changes backstage, thus giving an appearance, at least, of being able to face anything that comes. They speak of religion without God, transcendent humanity without religion and a whole range of bewildering attitudes so that people may be forgiven for wondering what faith it is or which way of life is being fulfilled. It is the way of the gnostic where esoteric understanding seems to preserve something even though it cannot be communicated to others.

We began this chapter, with the comforting support of Alasdair MacIntyre, by insisting that although intellectual truth is important it is not the only measure of what we mean by truth. Indeed, there is a real sense in which it is no adequate measure at all because it would leave on one side the vast majority of people. Perhaps those who consider themselves to be intellectual may find themselves disqualified because of the rule they so confidently selected. The Bible certainly points in this direction and it will be well to remember that what it says about truth is not as intellectual, even in the narrow sense, as the English words suggest. All this is bound up with the annoying habit of the Jew who insists on seeing man as a whole. It is annoying to us, because we are so used to separating man into body, soul and spirit. If we say that we have long since dismissed soul and spirit, we are then left only with a body and, not quite knowing what to do with it, we look anxiously towards psychiatrists and psychologists hoping that perhaps they may be able to breathe some true life into it.

This is not the place to discuss fully the biblical view of truth but I shall indicate some distinctions which are necessary for the preacher. A man may be urged to defend what is true much after the manner of Perry Mason – the difference being, as someone has said, that Mason wins all his cases. This explains how there has been a pulpit manner reminiscent of a lawyer tackling his brief. Following this fashion the preacher assembles his arguments, giving wide range to other possibilities, and then proceeds to knock down what was conveniently set up. He seals the solution of the problem before beginning to ask the questions. No one need be bewildered because it is clear from the beginning and on previous form that the conclusion of the dogmatic preacher will be sound. Thus he satisfies the faithful and himself but the imported jury may suspect that he has failed to make a case. Now the Greek mind would have little difficulty in responding to this method and this is the reason that preaching in this style has a long and distinguished pedigree. Truth, on this understanding, is timeless truth found in passing events. It is an eternal state possessed by the human mind but not always with the same brightness. It is not concrete but abstract; not in history but timeless. It is truth as opposed to falsehood, or reality as opposed to mere appearance.

The Hebrew, however, does not speak of truth as an impersonal state of affairs which may be resolved merely by discussion. For him truth is understood in terms of relationships and is bound with the prevailing Old Testament theme of covenant. Thus there are times when truth would be better translated as faith. The Hebrew word has the meaning of 'faithfulness, trustworthiness and sureness'. We can understand the confusion Pilate must have felt when he raised what for him must have sounded like a philosophical argument. Truth is not a stated concept which the intellect grasps so much as reality made known and received in personal relationships. The gospel word in Christ gives not only knowledge of the Christ but power to do the truth. This word of good news is always found in the relationships of people with each other and to treat it as an abstraction from life, to be legally applied, kills the spirit now as then.

In all this there is a great need for the preacher to be both honest and sympathetic. There are times when he faces a congregation of people who are still unshaken in their beliefs. Always there are some people able to live in this innocent assurance who are as blissfully unaware of the work of scholars as they seem to be of how the heathen rage. Their need is to be confirmed in the faith, and a blundering clergyman who is eager to stir the sediment of his own doubts is simply being offensive when he forgets where the people are. It does not seem to me to be a part of the preacher's job to trample over things which for so long have been considered sacred. There are also people who are in a crippling condition of bewildering doubt. Having heard rumours that the building in which they have lived is no longer secure they have no alternative place in which they can find shelter. And, again, there are those who having passed from innocent belief to nagging doubt are now waiting for the next stage in the pilgrimage. It is not a mark of maturity in any preacher when he wilfully ignores any one of these conditions. As a man himself he will not need to look upon them with objective interest. He need only scrape a little bit and he will uncover similar layers in his own experience.

6

Is the Bible True?

The modern era in preaching began when the Bible was made open to human inquiry. It all started innocently, so it seemed, with someone wanting to bite into the book instead of simply enjoying its promises. It was, in the human story, a fateful bite. What had appeared to be protected, divinely immune from grasping hands, became vulnerable. The effect of this simple exploration had a drastic effect on the message of the preacher. There grew a rift between those who imagined they could yet linger in the garden and those who were tempted to climb over the wall.

Protestants have sometimes imagined that they invented an inerrant Bible while the Catholics were celebrating in wayward traditional ways of their own devising. So it would be well to understand that there has been a long and complicated history bound to the idea of the inerrancy of scripture. There are three traditional ways in which the problem has been approached. The first was the most comforting when it was possible to attribute the writing of scripture to a small band of men. Moses had written the Pentateuch; Joshua the Book of Joshua; Samuel the Books of Samuel and so on, with David writing the Psalms and Solomon rather remarkably finding time to produce Proverbs, Wisdom, Ecclesiastes and the Song of Songs. Similarly with the New Testament. Eight sacred and inspired writers wrote all the books. Since all the books were composed in their final form the authors and the books had a common inspiration. The second formula regarding inerrancy accepted the possibility of a large number of anonymous writers, so that not only was the final form seen as inerrant but also those writers who, somewhat unwittingly, helped the process of fulfilment on its way. The third traditional way dealt with the 'inerrancy of the Bible' as a whole and spoke of the total statement of scripture. It will not be thought that the story was as simple and straightforward as I have made it appear. There were long centuries of discussion about authorship, exegesis and exposition but it will serve our purpose now to see that scripture was regarded as reliable and that the word of salvation is there. In the record of Vatican Council II there are some magnificent passages which save revelation from being restricted to truth in propositional forms and where communion with Christ rather than knowledge about him is emphasized. The discussion still goes on and one of the exciting experiences in the modern Roman Catholic church is the joy of the people in their new freedom to read the Bible.

It is possible to appreciate the importance of tradition in this attempt to understand the Bible. Protestants, however, do not easily forget that their own traditional emphasis on the value of reading the Bible was not encouraged by the Roman Catholic warnings about the perils arising from reading it with an untutored mind. Sometimes it seemed that there was a secret knowledge of an esoteric tradition, as with the scribes, which was given to the church in addition to the scriptures. Yet it is obvious that the Bible has been central in the whole story of the church. The Roman Catholic, however, gained an unfair advantage over the Protestant because he had not only an inerrant Bible but the source of inerrant interpretation as well.

We shall not understand the wilful reaction of fundamentalists at the very beginning of this century unless we can also recapture the earlier thrill men felt when the people heard the gospel for the first time in their own tongues. Men who had heard remnants of the Bible read in a foreign language and gazed at it chained in a sacred place were now given this word expounded in a new way. It is no wonder that people were excited about it, flocking to hear it in Calvin's Geneva or Elizabethan England. From that day preaching was not merely the eloquence of a man but the offering of the Word of God.

Since they and their children were nurtured on this for so long the first rumour of criticism must have been grievous news. It was the rumour, rather than any disciplined knowledge, which spread. And it was with a mingling of fear and horror that there came the determination to defend the truth.

It might be supposed that there is no difficulty in presenting the case for a dogmatic attitude to the Bible. But a little reflection shows that it is no easy thing. I have observed with interest that a dogmatic structure soon becomes open to varied interpretations. An interesting exercise would be to attempt to say what Karl Marx taught in the kind of straightforward digest such an attitude to life seems to demand. We soon discover that what one man says Marx taught differs considerably from the view of another. This is not necessarily because one knows while the other is ignorant. Indeed, both may claim to know only to discover that a third man comes along and says that both are wrong. Similarly with the verbal inspiration of the Bible. Let us say that Professor William Barclay of Glasgow is invited to explain this view to the hungry readers of a newspaper. He sits down to explain what seems perfectly obvious only to find that the resulting correspondence not only disagrees with what he has said but also amongst itself. Within the dogmatic structure there is room to manoeuvre, and sometimes opposing views are laid on the same foundation.

The problem is made even more confusing because of the term dogma. A Christianity without dogma is no Christianity at all. Students wishing to advertise their love of freedom and annoyed by the disagreements of former centuries may offer theses on a theology without dogma only to succeed in revealing their own ignorance. In the eleventh century St Anselm put it in this way: 'Just as the right order of going requires that we should believe the deep things of God before we presume to discuss them by reason, so it seems to me negligence if, after we have been confirmed in the faith, we do not study to understand what we believe.'[1] Dogmatic theology is born when doubt denies what has been affirmed. The heretic performs the service of encouraging the church to state its mind and when the church does this, other heretics appear who tell the church that the formulas are wrong. Heresy, therefore, should emerge from the love of the church – it is a response to the love which has been expressed in confessions of faith. Of course this love was sometimes displayed in peculiar ways, like burning the heretic. It may be asking too much of modern man to invite him to appreciate this strange method of showing affection but there were plenty of people who defended the procedure in earlier days. However, I simply want to underline the point that we do not get rid of the need for dogma by saying that we do not like it, nor of the heretic by pretending he no longer exists. In a discussion of this kind there is a necessary dialectic and the argument swings to and fro. In discussing fundamentalism I am not pretending to favour a faith or a view of the Bible which has no dogma. Dogma is necessary where there is an attempt to state what we believe; dogmatism is a perverse narrowing of the mind. The effort must be made to present dogma without being crudely dogmatic.

Yet the views of inerrancy of the Bible to which we have referred should not be equated with fundamentalism. The word finds its origin in a series of paperback booklets issued from the USA and which were entitled *The Fundamentals*.[2] In doctrine they were strictly conservative and I feel some familiarity with them because I remember as a boy reading them avidly with a view to understanding something about the beginning and the end of the world. The first was published in 1909 and the series dealt with questions of the early return of Christ, the substitutionary theory of the atonement, eternal punishment and kindred subjects as well as driving home a rigid doctrine of the verbal inerrancy of the Bible. In this view of the Bible there are similarities with an earlier view of scripture but the tone becomes more urgent because there is a determined disgust with the rise of biblical criticism. Yet it goes much further than this because, as distinct from Aquinas and Calvin, the authors insisted on the scientific accuracy of Genesis, thinking it unnecessary and unwise for people to go elsewhere, as Calvin advised, to 'learn astronomy and other recondite arts'. Or perhaps it is more accurate to say that any scientific exploring which contradicted Genesis was false. I must confess that I gained much comfort from this and it is no difficulty for me to recall now the relief I felt when a 'day' in creation could be understood as a long period of time, and when the true order of creation could be seen in Genesis although it had taken scientists so long to discover it! Scientists who produced something which could not be reconciled with the creation story in Genesis were roundly condemned. I felt that the trembling ground had become safe.

I have no doubt that this crude apologetic had an enormous influence in the early part of this century. So much so that when conservative scholars produced more subtle views they, too, appeared to be dabbling in novelties. There are still many remains of the views urged in *The Fundamentals*, particularly on the question of creation and the substitutionary view of the atonement. In general understanding in succeeding years, it was accepted that *any* text from the Bible had this nature of inspiration although there were vigorous efforts to harmonize discordant themes with each other. Whatever sophisticated conservative scholars may say, I trust the memory of the community in which I was nurtured. It was that you gave respect to any text wherever it was found and tried to see it for what it was, i.e. the word of God. Failure to achieve this impossible task produced a growing burden of guilt. The sense of guilt is with me still. This was similar to the common view of an infallible Bible, and the denial of it by some conservative scholars reminds me of the way in which Roman Catholic scholars assert that the church never taught, say, the worship of Mary only to find that nearly every common man thought it did.

Preachers fed by this kind of propaganda – and there were many of them – approached their congregation Sunday by Sunday and frequently during the week with confidence. Preachers and people seemed protected with an impregnable armour. Yet the more rumour and knowledge of other ways spread the more aggressive some of them became. The authors of *The Fundamentals*, including B. B. Warfield, Campbell Morgan and I believe A. T. Pierson, were men of piety and character but they set their followers in a later time an impossible task. It would be wrong to measure truth by sociological pressures but when the advance of knowledge moves relentlessly on it is foolish to try to sweep back the tide. This does not mean that knowledge is to be accepted uncritically but it does mean that it cannot be ignored or treated as an enemy because the mind has already become fixed in faith. Let me give one quotation from a book published by the Evangelical Press which illustrates this: 'The Bible, it is true, is not a scientific textbook; but if it is true, it is true on every level, and is the divinely given framework of all knowledge.'[3]

Before trying to assess the significance of all this for preaching it should be recognized that the view expressed in *The Fundamentals* is not entirely common to conservative interpretation. Conservatives also change. Anglicans of a rare kind have told me that they do not share the more vitriolic spirit of some of my Baptist brethren. Since my purpose is simply to consider the strength and weakness of this position in preaching I have no wish to be too playful about the difficulty of unravelling a knot which one would expect to be of a simple kind. But I know from experience that apparent simplicity can be most complicated. A few years ago I thought it would be good to encourage some united study of the Bible and Christian doctrine. So in my innocence I chose several scholars as possible expositors of a biblical theme. One was a professor whose books stand alongside Spurgeon on the shelves of Russian Baptist ministers, but he was summarily rejected. Another lecturer, offered tentatively, came from a college of impeccable orthodoxy – so I thought. His candidature came to a sudden end when one of the ministers on the committee raised his hands in the posture of an ancient curse and said 'My people wouldn't stand for him.' At this point I determined to withdraw with what little grace I could muster and since that day I have remained in cowardly retreat from this kind of educational enterprise.

But let me give one more example of a more enlightened yet still bewildering sort. It comes from Gresham Machen. I choose him because he was familiar to me at the beginning of my college course. The book was published in 1936 but I have a right to expect a not too rapid change in the habits of conservatives. After all I am not dealing with existential blushes.

Machen writes:

> I hold that the Biblical writers, after having been prepared for their task by the providential ordering of their entire lives, received, in addition to all that a blessed and wonderful and supernatural guidance and impulsion by the Spirit of God, so that they were preserved from the errors that appear in other books and thus the resulting book, the Bible, is in all its parts the very Word of God, completely true in what it says regarding matters of fact and completely authoritative in its commands.[4]

Machen goes on to say that he is not attributing plenary inspiration to any translation nor yet to the thousands of Greek and Hebrew manuscripts, for these were the work of copyists. Only the books from the pens of the sacred writers had this supernatural quality. But Machen recognizes that though the copyists erred they were doing God's work. He insists that all parts of the Bible are not equally alike or equally beautiful 'or even equally valuable; but . . . all parts of the Bible are equally true, and that each part has its place'.

Whenever people have a book as the fount of their faith there is this problem of asserting its authority and the authentic quality of its composition. Although I cannot submit to the logic of Gresham Machen I can appreciate the need for assurance on the nature of the text and its transmission. Similar concerns can be found in discussions about the Koran or the statements about 'sruti' in relation to the sacred Vedic literature when the human ear receives the divine voice, handing on the message by word of mouth or pen. Here, too, the sacred books are guarded with a jealousy which the most mechanical conceptions of biblical inspiration have rarely equalled. In addition, as far as Hinduism is concerned, we have the example of Radhakrishnan re-interpreting the idea of 'sruti'. We have seen that throughout the history of the church there has been a deep desire to guard the Bible from assault and Gresham Machen's defence has some interesting links with the whole story.

We have now to ask ourselves whether the work of critical study on the Bible has in fact destroyed the power both of the preacher and the book. We must confess that sometimes it appears to be so. Just as the fundamentalist was seen to be excessive in his defence operations, so the new critic looked like a man facing the world naked, brandishing a wooden sword. It is easy to caricature a man armed with critical apparatus enlarging on possible forms of composition and then forgetting what he meant to say. I think there can be no doubt that the trumpet call was muted and men had no idea where they were supposed to march. I should admit, somewhat grudgingly, that the conservative has performed a great service by insisting that there must be a message, without it being hedged around with all kinds of qualifications and suppositions. Genuine doubt and struggling are not the same thing as no message at all. It is also clear to me that the Bible is a unique witness to the God of history. Without this there is no abiding word and, certainly, experience, standing alone, will neither recreate the vitality of the past nor open a way for the future. The church also is lost without the witness of the Bible and it can inflate itself as much as it likes but it will be to no avail. Pronouncements and resolutions by the church at best seem to be of doubtful value but without the faith kindled by the light of the Bible they will be entirely futile. Any authority of the church and the preacher lies ultimately in the Bible. It is there that we hear of the story to be told and what H. H. Farmer called 'the sheerly objective, historical, undeserved givenness, which the Christian revelation claims for itself.'

The modern attitude to the Bible and therefore the sermon often sounds a different note. The story is not told and there is much doubt about whether there is a story to tell. It is like Samuel Beckett's play, *Krapp's Last Tape*. Krapp sits there listening over and over to old speeches he had taped many years ago and he is unable to make any sense out of them. He is cut off from the past, even his own past. The preacher finds himself in a similar position and, being modern, he starts talking about his own place, London or New York or wherever it may be. This is a way highly commended today and there is much to be said for it. But he can be discursive on London without ever arriving in Bethlehem, Nazareth or Calvary. That is where the story is lost because the preacher has no remembrance of things past. It is not a question of going back but of experiencing a living remembrance as people have done through centuries at the Lord's Table. If one aspect of our condition is that the preacher forgets to tell the story, the other side is that the congregation has no hunger for it. Men do not feed on the word, as once they did, nor on the bread and wine. Kafka's story 'The Fasting Showman' tells of a showman who earned much curiosity by abstaining from food. People came from far and near to see his almost fleshless body. In time they tired of the act but the showman, dying, whispered his secret – there was simply no food he ever liked. The modern situation regarding preaching is that people suspect that they have preachers who have forgotten the story. The people themselves dwell in a land where there is a famine of the word and where even the desire for food has died.

7

The Yarrow Blossom

Historical criticism of the Bible, as we have seen, produced widespread alarm in the nineteenth century. It seemed as though sceptical scholars were tampering with the word of God. Although the word 'criticism' had been a technical term for centuries, referring to variant manuscript readings, it had sinister significance in the new situation. The attempt to deal with the Bible on the lines of modern literary and historical methods aroused suspicion and this only increased when hidden sources of the Bible were explored and various continental scholars tried to trace the development of oral tradition. All this belongs to the modern study of the Bible but to understand the place of the preacher in this story we must see the human reasons that lay behind the alarm.

It is important to remember that, on any measurement of time, the beginning of the controversy was not long ago. The Robertson Smith case illustrates this. His article on the Bible appeared in the *Encyclopaedia Britannica* in December 1875. At that time he was just thirty years of age. His concern was strictly critical and while dealing historically with the text of the Bible he yet found it possible to remain a Calvinist and an evangelical with a proper respect for the Westminster Confession. It was the separation of questions of dogma from scholarly criticism that made it possible for some, at least, to find their balance after the shock they had received. Smith in fact was, unwittingly, opening fields of scholarship which even he had not perceived. He went back to Semitic origins of Hebrew beliefs and customs and thus went beyond Wellhausen who was primarily concerned with the Old Testament itself. Yet his faith, as his friends realized, was firmly grounded and this assured him of the strong support of men like Alexander Whyte. This brings us to the period after the First Great War because Whyte lived from 1836–1921. We must remember that we are so near to the shaking of the foundations that we ourselves should feel the ground still trembling.

In this short period of time the sweep of biblical scholarship has been immense. It is difficult to think of any other scholarly activity comparable with it. Beginning with a searching investigation of literature and religion it also dealt with the origin of religion. Archaeological and language research added to the growing discipline, and scholars becoming dissatisfied with the early reconstructions began to speak of patterns and myths in the ancient world which were assumed to shed light on great movements in biblical tradition, like the Exodus story. Yet again there was the examination of a long period of oral tradition with an attempt to give some chronological shape to the Old Testament books which finally emerged. The debate about the date of the various books of the Old Testament still goes on. It is, indeed, difficult to find any significant period which is not a subject of controversy. The impatient are inclined to regret so much labour and others are fearful lest the living book should be lost in the select studies of the scholars. This fear is understandable and it is found among the scholars themselves as well as in the common Christian man. I was greatly comforted by a number of conversations with Theodore Robinson (of the famous Oesterley & Robinson partnership). On one occasion I asked him what changes he would make if he rewrote his *History of Israel.*[1] He gave me a long look and then murmured rather impatiently that he would make none. It was the comment of an old man who had grown tired and rather bewildered about those who worked over the same ground with modern machines.

It should not take long to realize, whatever may be the mood of elderly scholars, that once the scientific study of scripture had begun there could be no retreat. If the preacher is anxious to get at the great themes of the Old Testament he may well do so in a simple frontal attack but he is bound to recognize, in time, that the ideas themselves have a way of escaping when separated from the historical setting. We may grumble as much as we like but the way of study will be pursued if only because, like Everest, it is there to be climbed. You need not be old to reflect that there was a time when Oesterley and Robinson, Wheeler Robinson and Adolph Lods seemed to have opened every possible Old Testament door. There were other names and some older, venerable ones but these I have mentioned could be guaranteed to lead stumbling students through any examination. Now, Eichrodt, Gerhard von Rad, Claus Westermann and a multitude of other scholars have brought a wealth of new insights and knowledge. In this modern scene, marked by the complication of ancient tongues with academic scholars roaming the desert and chipping at archaeological sites, the preacher stands in the pulpit to offer the Word of God. What possible relevance has all this industry got for him? Some withdrew from the battlefield before they really arrived. Others started with eager zeal but discovering they had some academic gifts found themselves stuck in Semitic roots. There are still others who feel in their bones the excitement which comes from research but they are not able, adequately, to deal with it and after some years feel utterly lost. What had seemed a Word of God disappeared like morning mist. The preacher, moreover, must bear in mind not only his own competence but the needs of a congregation who hear of scholarship only through occasional sensations in the daily press. If the preacher is blandly intellectual he will soon find himself delivering a monologue which he alone hears. If he is wilfully blind to scholarship he will in time become effective only to the dying and the dead. How is he to give a word to the living?

There are a number of ways in which this is attempted Sunday by Sunday, but the Old Testament presents peculiar problems because there is much controversy about the relationship between the Old and the New Testaments. However, let us suppose for the moment that a preacher intends dealing with the Old Testament. If his mind is crippled by problems, he is not likely to get far. The most serious difficulty is that the imagination is stifled. Intending to be honest he finds himself rooted in the ancient world, unable to move because he is not sure where he is or where he hoped to go. The date of Exodus enthralls him so that when eventually he tells the people to go forward the walls of water have already collapsed. If the Old Testament is to be used in preaching, the one thing that matters is that there should be a message. The pulpit is not the place for a man to display his academic knowledge. The sermon is justified only if it brings a word from God. There are other forms of instruction which are beneficial, though unable to make this outrageous claim. But the sermon makes this claim and it does so not as a boastful aside but as the very reason for its delivery. Talks and literary essays are not sermons and the sermon is bound indissolubly with the book which the preacher uses. No other book, however inspirational, can take the place of this book. It is the one book and it either contains the revealing word of God or it does not. A sermon based on such a book will not only be spoken, it must be seen to perform and do the work about which the message speaks.

It is clear, therefore, that before we can consider how justified the claim may be in terms of the Old Testament, we should know what the Old Testament is saying. Here I have found much help in the recent writings of J. N. Schofield, who was one of my tutors at university. Schofield, formerly a Lecturer in Hebrew and Old Testament studies at Leeds and Cambridge universities, was President of the Society for Old Testament Study in 1969. My early memory of him is of a man immersed in Ras Shamra and living as one ready to die for an unorthodox date of the book of Deuteronomy. He knows all about critical and pattern approaches to Old Testament study and made his own contribution in *The Historical Background of the Bible*[2] and *The Religious Background of the Bible*.[3] In a more recent book, *Law, Prophets and Writings*,[4] Schofield acknowledges his debt to Otto Procksch, Walther Eichrodt, H. H. Rowley and Gerhard von Rad and then proceeds to deal with the final form of the Hebrew Old Testament as the basis of his study. Introductions to the various books and comments on difficult sections of the text become subservient to the word itself. It is in fact the way in which Bonhoeffer discovered the wealth of the Old Testament – by letting the word speak. Schofield uses the picture of the yarrow blossom to illustrate his method. The yarrow, with stems of varying length, produces a magnificent spreading flower-head on the same plane. It is the 'whole flower' which is presented and the glory of Old Testament religion is offered in the form given by the final editors.

In dealing in this way with the Old Testament only, the Christian preacher, if he allowed himself to be so restricted, would suffer considerable strain. He does not endure this conflict because in his mind the Old Testament is read and understood in terms of the Christian faith. We are trying to look at the two Testaments separately because it is expedient to do so. The modern preacher's temptation is not to make too much of the Old Testament but virtually to ignore it altogether. In Free Church services it is still quite common to find a New Testament lesson only, and if there are two lessons the Old Testament lesson is not used as the source of the text. In a study group to which I belong we decided to give a session to 'Preaching the Old Testament today'. Dr Henton Davies, the Principal of Regent's Park College, Oxford, was invited to introduce the subject. We discovered that in many churches it was a notable occasion if anyone chose to preach from the Old Testament. The book, although full of delightful stories, was viewed as an embarrassment in the pulpit. There is some traditional support for this reserve. Luther, for example, preached much more from New Testament texts than from the Old and he claimed that 'the Old Testament is not to be preached'. It is possible to take the view that while preaching from the Old Testament is not permissible it is right and essential to use it as the background for the presentation of the gospel.[5]

Bultmann is a central figure in this discussion as in so much of the modern study of the Bible. He is of particular interest here because although he does not hold that the Old Testament is revelation for a Christian he still makes it possible for the book to enrich and even create understanding. His emphasis is on pre-understanding (*Vorverständnis*) which makes it possible, for example, to have a response to love, joy and forgiveness simply because these call out something which is already a part of human experience. There is an understanding of history because there is some prior understanding in one's own life.

The Old Testament story, in this sense, with its portrayal of characters gradually emerging into clarity, gives understanding in the way in which our own lives and motives become visible to us. There is not only a link with our lives but the creation of a correspondence which calls forth a pre-understanding to which the Christian proclamation may speak. This may be illustrated in the way in which Thomas Mann on Joseph and Dan Jacobson on Tamar help us to grasp our own historical situation as they tell a story of long ago. Or, more directly, there is the example of Bultmann himself preaching on Genesis 8.22 – 'While earth remains, seed time and harvest, cold and heat, summer and winter, day and night shall not cease' – in Germany during 1937. Or, again, Gerhard Ebeling reading Isaiah 14 to non-church colleagues at the time of a rumour about the death of Hitler. It was not difficult for those who were unfamiliar with the Bible to take the step from Babylon to their own situation. Here Old Testament history is also an understanding of one's own life.

To Bultmann, however, the Old Testament is not indispensable because other literature may be used as a preface to the New Testament. I can see that there is a good deal of psychological validity in this kind of approach but I must confess that it is not mine. I am encouraged by the considerable differences in the way scholars explain the significance of the Old Testament. Literature and myths, both old and new, are windows which give light to New Testament truth but, in practice, the preacher is most effective when he refuses to play fast and loose with the canon of the Old Testament as with the New. It is perilously easy for people to assess literature by its capacity to move as though we were dealing with the fitful changes of top of the pops. Preachers will occasionally read from Wesley or William Temple or even the Mahabharata in the tone of voice which suggests that they have discovered a new scripture. Sometimes extravagance encourages them to read from less worthy people simply because they were touched by a piece of prose or poetry the week before. In doing this they will argue, if challenged, that they find these choice selections more full of 'inspiration' than Leviticus. This may well be so but the sermon gives a man liberty to offer the fruits of his reading.

Yet the historical witness of scripture does not depend upon its immediate inspiration and power to move the hearts of men. Like the Chosen People, it cannot be replaced by something else simply because it falls below Wordsworth, W. H. Auden or Patience Strong. Respect for Israel and reverence for the God of Israel urge me to be as firm in resisting these novelties as I should be about similar treatment of the books of the New Testament. The absurdities into which we may be led by ignoring this warning were illustrated for me in a multi-faith service in my own church at Bloomsbury. I should justify this occasional mixed act of witness on a number of grounds and I do not feel it should be despised because it can lead to misunderstanding. On this occasion we had an act of meditation in which some Hindu texts and sacred syllables were repeated. The leader had a superb voice and with the help of amplifiers he created a sense of awe in a sympathetic and receptive congregation. I have no doubt that it was helpful to those in the same tradition but to my surprise it was spoken of afterwards by some of the Christians as the most effective contribution of the evening. It reminded me of H. H. Farmer's comment about a man mistaking the oscillation of his diaphragm in harmony with a ten-foot organ pipe for a visitation of the Holy Spirit. So I am not greatly attracted to moving music, poetry or prose as a substitute for scripture. It is not the sort of *Vorverständnis* which creates faith nor prepares the way for it.

No one, I hope, is going to attribute these absurdities to Bultmann, but the preacher will be wise not to let Shakespeare or any great literary figure blind him to the different nature of the biblical record. I take it that when we speak of the scriptures we are referring to something unique and it is not to be measured by literary taste. If it were, then there is much in the Bible which could be rejected. There is today a special reason for this insistence. The advent of critical scholarship made it appear as though we were not talking about a message which is of unique significance. In the conflict with those who were suspicious of any modern scholarly activity there were some who treated the Bible as though it were only a record of ancient customs of nothing but historic and academic interest. It is not surprising that in scholarship as in life there is light and shade.

The shadows cast were deep and full of gloom because they seemed to come from the setting of a great light. Yet for me, as for many others, the insights of study brought a new light and I have never forgotten how the Bible came alive for me in ways I had not anticipated. This, of course, is what we should expect, because if we are dealing with a text it ought to be some advantage to know what we are talking about. It is surely impossible not to be helped by what Norman Snaith calls the distinctive ideas of the Old Testament where the holiness of God, the righteousness of God, the salvation of God, the covenant-love and election-love of God, the salvation of God, yield fresh meanings as men become aware both of the roots and the subsequent growth. This, as we shall see in the next chapter, is not all that needs to be done but it is an important and essential beginning in the work of the preacher. It must not be supposed that those who did not have these benefits were left in the dark. The position, as I see it, is like the Froebel approach to education, that each generation receives what it requires. 'Henry's Bible' and Edersheim still hold much that is valuable and a wisdom which does not wither with age, but it would be foolish to pretend that we are being the more loyal to them by ignoring Manson and Jeremias. It is high time that those who have received so much from the labour of others should openly rejoice in what has been given.

It is possible for some to argue that scholarship has given nothing. The ways of men, like those of God, can be mysterious. Yet if this argument is persistent we need to be aware of the nature of this claim. It could be a defence of ignorance as though the faith can flourish only when we are blind to the facts. This is not a position to be envied nor is it improved when we act as though we could be selective, choosing what supports our case and rejecting whatever may oppose it. This still remains a deceiving way and no man can abide it for long without something valuable in his life being destroyed. Pretending to follow the truth, he is living a lie. It is also possible that the research of the scholar will show that the faith is hollow. This, I think, is the hidden fear. But if this is truly the result of modern biblical scholarship then there can be no doubt about what an honest man should do.

Biblical scholarship, however, is not restricted to a search for history and an examination of literary records. Even people who are not persuaded by the claims of faith must surely go beyond this unless they wish to be offensive to the subject of their studies. They may, of course, say that having looked at the ideas and values they remain unimpressed or have no wish to be counted with such people. This seems to be fair enough and I have no desire to encourage any man to surrender a comfortable chair simply because he is unwilling to be reckoned as a believer. I assume that any man who wants to study ancient records as a way of earning a living may do so even though he may despise the people and customs he studies. There are instances of men who have done this with apparent effect and people who have gained degrees on the same grounds. But for the man of faith it will be quite different. He will not be satisfied with academic gymnastics alone nor even with uncovering a few interesting ideas which may have some relevance for today. A scholar who is involved in this way may be accused of bias. This was an accusation frequently flung at Jewish and Christian scholars in their reaction to the Dead Sea Scrolls. Edmund Wilson, for example, seemed to imply that any 'believer' was so biassed that it was impossible for him to be objective. The only alternative was that atheists would have to learn the language so that people could get a proper view of things. A scholar, wanting to be objective, would be right to claim that he was studying his material with a fair mind and that his fellow scholars must be trusted to respect his integrity. He would be placed in an awkward position if he had to deny his convictions in order to appear impartial. A preacher certainly cannot be limited in this way. It may be unfortunate that the story of Israel is so closely linked with a living faith that it is not easy to study it as one might the religion of Mithras. But in studying it – this is the nature of the case – a man must make it clear where he stands in relation to its contemporary appeal. The preacher is a man who has made up his mind, whether he is a serious student or not.

When a man of faith seeks to interpret the story of Israel he may find that the people on whom he relies for an understanding of the texts differ among themselves in the emphasis they make. I want to give a personal view of the Old Testament message which owes a good deal to a variety of people. In summary it will cut out much that is of value but there is a theme that prevails, as I understand it, and which often appears in my preaching.

The story of Israel tells of a people who set out to live their lives under God. Since it is difficult to imagine them deciding to do such a thing, as though it were an easy way of living, we are confronted by the election-love of God which chooses Israel not for prestige but for service. They were chosen to receive the revelation of God, to reflect the character of God and for service to the world. It is God who chooses and he is recognized by the people when they are open to his coming. Punished and purged, the people are prepared for a mission to the world. The God who does this is not visible to inquisitive eyes. Indeed he spends a good deal of the time hiding himself (Ex. 3; Isa. 8.16–17; Ps. 74). Yet the reality of God, present and absent, is the pre-supposition of experience and thought. It is the 'fool' who lives as though God could be ignored.

This God is known by what he does in history. Nature religions which promise salvation through the natural rhythms of life are a lie. Baal and Ashtart were not gods of history nor was Chemosh of Moab. These were not the gods who had brought Israel out of Egypt and made a covenant with her – though kings might try to deceive the people and urge a religion of convenience (I Kings 12.28). The Old Testament speaks of God in historical experience and of history with God. The central thought of covenant makes it clear that any relationship between God and his people is preceded by what God has done (Deut. 26.5–10). Election-love and covenant-love are not a celebration of love for all men in general and none in particular. They are like a mother's love for her child – unconditional, persistent, unfailing, steadfast. What God has done and continues to do calls forth a faith which endures through destruction of the sanctuary, political extinction, exile and even the rebellious way of those who were called into the covenant. Through heart-breaking strain and stress the faith lives, stronger than death, that God is the Lord of history and his purpose will be fulfilled for all mankind.

Thus Israel is to remember, to re-tell, to live her story as a way of faith. Yet when the story was told as though God were confined to the past history of his people, there was a prophet to hand who told them of the God whose deliverance was also for the people of a new day. (Isa. 43; Deut. 5.3). They looked along dark corridors and saw a great light. The conviction remains constant even when it is limited to a few – 'God is with us' (Isa. 7.14; Hos. 11.9; Amos 5.14). It is easy to see all this in the prophets but what is of even greater significance is the way in which this is celebrated in the festal days of worship. The Horeb–Siniai covenant, reaffirmed in the House of David, enshrines a great hope. Although gods of nature cannot save, there is no doubt that the God of history is in control of the natural world as of the lives of men on the plane of history, and always the hope abides of fulfilment in a world of righteousness and peace.

We must remember that the books of the Old Testament cover a long period of history – say from the Norman Conquest to today – and there is much about the way in which the growing predicament of man in selfishness, futility and guilt spoiled the earth which was his home. But always there is the continuing purpose of God in his mighty acts for a rebellious people. This is the story to be told and the drama to be presented. It is this which the preacher must proclaim until, in exile and return, the covenant binds people to God and to each other. We proclaim not simply a tale of long ago, as though there were no living remembrance of things past, but the story which sets every man on stage under a blazing light. I have heard that in one of Von Schlegel's plays the curtain rises to show the inside of a theatre where an audience is waiting for the curtain to rise. As it does the audience sees another audience gazing expectantly at a curtain. The second curtain rises and reveals a similar scene so that the first audience looks anxiously over its shoulder to see if it too is on stage.

I always hope that my Jewish friends will allow me to share something of their story as it has been received by them. This, of course, cannot be the end of the story for me. Indeed the end of the story has not yet been told for any man of any faith. There is a sense in which one does not speak of the end, for terminal language of this kind can but wait on the new creation. So I recall the times I have worshipped in synagogues and shared the sense of reverence when the scrolls of the Law are brought from their sacred place and presented before the people. One occasion I remember with special feeling. It was a day when the reading told of the way opened through the Red Sea. My fellow worshippers, all Jews, included many people from Europe and some of them remembered a time when there had been no escape. Yet they celebrated, still, like men with an undying hope and I am sure I saw the water dripping from their hats. It was not the memory of a distant date in history which held them because they too were experiencing Exodus and rejoicing in the covenant.

8

A Risky Business

In considering the task of the preacher in relation to the Old Testament we have emphasized the way in which the book is rooted in history. Some may well feel that this has been done too rashly and that we are in danger of landing ourselves in a biblicism from which we had seemed to escape. I must confess that I do not fear that danger. In my own experience the temptation has been to soften historical claims and to welcome other ways of interpretation. Yet the preacher, whatever his own inclinations may be, has inherited a historical faith. That fact is inescapable. Let him do what he may with the Christ of faith and the story of Israel but if he avoids the question of history he has surrendered the faith of his fathers, however worthy any substitute may be.

In terms of the Old Testament it is possible to combine the search for accurate information and devotion to the critical method without losing the significant themes. Scholars may debate the date of Exodus and differ by some hundreds of years and still proclaim the meaning of Exodus in theological harmony. Yet there is the sense in which the events are not merely folk-tales but the record of a history which the people celebrate. It was more comforting when a preacher could rely on the famous dating of Archbishop Usher and the Schofield Bible, but arguments about dates do not of themselves sever the faith from history. A preacher is not seriously limited if taking a text from Deuteronomy he is not happy about the date he could give it. Some dating is, of course, a real advantage because it enables him to have some better understanding of the historical background. But all this, while helpful, is not a matter of vital concern.

When the preacher comes to the New Testament he is immediately confronted by a much sharper problem. The background and occasion of gospels and epistles may not trouble him greatly and he is not likely to be distressed if he cannot make up his mind about which letters are assuredly Pauline. His anxiety is not so much about dates as about the fact of Jesus. Supposing he is ignorant about the dating of the gospels and the recognized sources, he may yet give his message with conviction. He will be happy in the thought that however late they may be he is on much surer ground than a Buddhist who has some four hundred years' gap between the probable time of the Buddha's life and the recording of it. The Buddhist, as it happens, has learned to live with this historical uncertainty and this marks a considerable difference between the two faiths. For the Christian the knowledge that Mark's gospel is a first century document is a piece of evidence which he should not lightly yield.

The modern preacher has been at the centre of the discussion about history even when he has not been aware of any conflict. Some have clung to historical certainty as a man clings to a raft. The Jesus of history has been so important to them that they have refused to countenance any scrutiny of the story of his life. While this is a commendable loyalty it is bound to lead in time to disappointment and, possibly, despair. The Christian way can never be confirmed by a wilful disregard of true evidence. This is but a longing for primitive innocence and it leads inevitably to the kind of aggression against honest scholarship which we have already witnessed. It does this because the matter in hand is of supreme importance and it is woefully easy to try to defend it by devious means. We are more concerned now with those who, while holding the faith, are troubled by doubts. This has been the mood of many in recent generations. The sword which was once held so firmly and which seemed to be blade-straight for the right has been snatched from the hand.

In this situation there has been a variety of responses. There was the passing confidence when people thought they could both confirm the facts about Jesus and discover new ones by diligent scholarship. Although the gospels could not properly be described as biographies it was yet felt that by persistent search a scholar would one day write the life and death of Jesus in a way acceptable to all. The only result was a series of bewildering 'lives' which often contradicted each other and merely reflected the aims and age of the writers themselves. The gentle Jesus, the idealist, the fanatic, the superman, the revolutionary, the rebel . . . there seemed to be no end to the possibilities. In some ways this variety showed the wealth in the subject being pursued but it also suggested that the text could be pressed into any desired shape producing a man or, possibly, a monster. The extravagance in this seems to have grown with the years. Harnack, for example, attempted to deal with the Jesus of history although he himself was well aware that the fourth gospel could not be taken as a historical authority in the ordinary meaning of the word, nor for that matter the synoptics. They were written not to give 'the facts as they were' but for 'work of evangelization'. Yet Harnack was attacked, on historical grounds, by the French modernist Abbé Loisy for presenting Jesus in terms which would make him acceptable to a scientific age. Where careful scholarship led to this kind of divergence it was even more likely that people starting deliberately with some preconceived idea of Jesus should encourage contradictions. When the preacher was constantly told that it was not possible to get at the bare facts of how things actually happened, it should not be difficult to sense his perplexity. The preacher had to give his sermon to a mixed congregation who were unaware of what went on in academic halls. He was sorely tempted to act as though nothing had changed.

In this setting there developed the view that it is the preaching of the Christ which matters. This solution to inevitable historical scepticism has been offered in different ways. It has within it an abiding validity but in recent times there has also been an attempt to be assured of the history within the kerygma. At first – about the beginning of this century – it was regarded by some as spiritually indecent to be inquisitive about the life of Jesus because the longing for guaranteed historical facts was in itself a denial of faith. The conclusion of this seemed to be that it would be best to have no history at all. But the emphasis on faith persisted. The sermon, so it was claimed, was direct address demanding faith. As Bultmann put it: 'Everything depends upon the Church's awareness of this in its preaching, that it may really strike the hearer as direct address in his concrete situation, so that he knows himself questioned, challenged, comforted, so that he cannot draw back.'[1] For Bultmann, preaching of this nature cannot be questioned – it is the simple challenge to faith.

There can be no doubt, whatever else has to be said, that this approach to preaching has been of great influence in the modern church. It is not always appreciated that Bultmann, like Barth, thought of his theology in terms of proclamation. The Lutheran influence is seen in this where the sermon represents the central function of the church. This emphasis grew when the human stage, particularly on the continent, became the scene of so much that was brutal and inhuman. Only a strong message could live in the face of so much ugly enmity and there were many who responded to a religion where the pattern in the life of Christ could be directly experienced, by faith, in contemporary human life. Presumably this 'existential' understanding would have been strengthened if it had been possible to link this experience of reconciliation and new life with reliable historical facts. But both on grounds of scholarship and by the nature of faith this was judged a futile quest. Preachers who rebel against the theology which lies behind this approach to the pulpit should not be unwilling to recognize the strength it gave to people in dark days. Nowhere is this more clearly seen than in the teaching of Bonhoeffer about preaching and the sermon. Having defended Bultmann against what he considered shameful attacks he also refused to become his disciple. Indeed there are hints which suggest that he wanted to go further than Bultmann but it is not clear in which direction he hoped to move. On the subject of the sermon, however, Bonhoeffer's foundation is firm although at one time in his life he regarded a preacher's seminary as a place to be avoided. He discouraged the temptation to discuss any sermon preached before a congregation, allowing only that there were rare private occasions when this might be done. 'Trust to the Word', he used to say. 'It is a ship loaded to the very limits of her capacity.' For him the word of the Bible assumed form as a sermon. He even pleaded, rather surprisingly, that there should be a tempting attraction in the sermon. It should be like a lovely red apple, held out to a child with the question 'Would you like it? . . .' 'Thus we should be able to speak about our faith so that hands will be stretched out towards us faster than we can fill them.'[2] So he encouraged his students not to argue or defend but to testify, combining in his teaching assertion with scepticism about the historic Jesus.

It is a great comfort to the preacher to know that a new generation of scholars came along and began to probe with disciplined minds into the problems which perplexed the common Christian. There was an intuitive desire to know more about Jesus and when some of the pupils of Bultmann began a new quest for the historical Jesus the hopes of many were raised. There was good reason for this because if there is more to be known and new ways of discovering it then this, in itself, is a sound reason for doing it. Much of this new exploration was carried out by gifted people who have instruments and tools not readily available to all. If the new approach was to be appreciated it meant that the preacher would have to rely upon the integrity of scholars like Bornkamm, Käsemann, C. H. Dodd and Jeremias. It must not be supposed that these agreed with one another, but they certainly represent a new attitude. Bultmann believed that there were a good number of things which could be known about Jesus but he emphasized the little we know and did not regard this as being of supreme importance. The later[3] teachers have been inclined to wonder that the little should be so much. Moreover they were eager to discover the meaning behind the events for those who were involved in them and tended not to lay so much emphasis, as in earlier times, on the 'bare facts'. It would be unwise to expect a biography of Jesus from this new inquiry but there is unquestionably a recognition that the tradition is more trustworthy than had once been assumed. C. H. Dodd's portrait of *The Founder of Christianity* is now widely known. Jeremias gives a picture of Jesus which is remarkably full, from the early days of the proclamation of Jesus to his death and resurrection. Even more surprising are the strong assertions of Wolfhart Pannenberg. He is significant because his name has sometimes been used by other scholars to frighten children in the conservative nursery. Yet Pannenberg says that the distinguishing fact about the Christian faith is that it is based essentially on historical events and a historical figure. He dismisses all attempts to replace the hazards of historical knowledge by the experience of faith or by the Christian 'kerygma' being interpreted primarily as a new understanding of existence. 'All these attempts are mere flights from the fact that Christian faith rests on its connection with a historical figure and on certain historical events.'[4]

There are some who will feel that this slight outline of the search for historical assurance is unnecessarily tortuous. They will wonder why we simply cannot accept the New Testament as it stands and have done with debate. This way is possible only for those who dislike the whole progress of critical scholarship. I can simply say that it is important for the preacher to recognize what has been taking place in biblical scholarship because the questions have been raised and because there has been some attempt to deal with them. We have seen that there have been considerable changes in the way in which scholars look at history and it should not be supposed that theologians have planned these in order to get themselves out of a problem. Indeed, developing ways of looking at the Jesus of history are reflected in the way in which historians have considered their craft. J. B. Bury's inaugural lecture at Cambridge in 1903 argued that 'history is a science, no less and no more'. It was expected that the historian, by claiming the method of a severe discipline, would uncover a record of bare facts unspoiled by any artistic flair for individual interpretation. Yet Harold Temperley, a friend and disciple of Bury, in his own 1930 inaugural lecture at Cambridge asserted that 'in my own memory the idea that history is a science has perished'. Thus history and interpretation came together in an indissoluble union, not because there was a desire to escape from scientific disciplines but because there was no other way of reading the past. Yet it is also clear that what we may call the scientific spirit – searching, questing, analysing, sifting – is a necessary part of any inquiry about the truth of things. In terms of the Christian faith this means that we must aim at the surest possible knowledge about Jesus. Apart from this willingness to be open to whatever is made known or discovered we shall be at the mercy of interpretations divorced from history where preachers proclaim the message of Christ which has nothing to do with Jesus. This may be possible for a Hindu who has absorbed 'the Christ' into his scheme of things, but it hardly seems a legitimate way for a Christian preacher.

The place of history, therefore, for the preacher is an important one. This is simply the nature of the case. If he is able to rely on a doctrine of inspiration which confirms both his beliefs and prejudices then he may count himself to be in a fortunate position. But infallible inspiration of this kind puts him in much the same position as a Moslem with the Koran and a Hindu with the Vedas. Presumably if the three met together they would spend an eternity of time asserting in a loud voice their respective claims. On this basis alone there would be nothing more that they could do about it. But history allied with interpretation gives greater flexibility to evangelism and to the act of proclamation. The preacher is not called merely to assert reliable events in the past. He is not even commissioned to argue or defend a case for what happened 2,000 years ago. A lecturer may do this when facts are assembled and reasons given for some conclusion about a way of life long ago. The preacher's task is more difficult. He has to span the wide chasm of history so that the once living word may come alive again to contemporary men and women. He must do this without letting the word be corrupted on the long journey, humanly speaking, and without being disloyal to the story which has been handed on. For the preacher, the primitive gospel must be understood as it is addressed to modern man.

The importance of a faith rooted in history may be seen when we contrast history and nature. This is a sharp philosophical problem and I have no ambition to make a sure judgment on an argument which has divided philosophers for many years. But nature does not interpret life. Learned men who have marvelled at an impression of design in nature refuse to accept it as evidence of design. If you come to nature with an experience of God you can speak of the God of Grace and the God of nature as one God. If you come without the initial faith you may marvel without being led to worship. In this the prophet (Isa. 40.25f.) and the psalmist (Ps. 8) are far removed from most modern men. The scientist, both in theory and technological possibility, looks at nature in a different way from the prophet and psalmist. Where the scientist sets out to *explain*, the doctrine of creation *interprets*. It is not so much a question of how things began but what is the meaning of things. History brings meaning into life. 'Acts of God', in flood or lightening, are understood by insurance companies as meaningless events but they become significant in history when they indicate, to an interpreting mind, God's way with men. A flash of lightening drives Martin Luther into a monastery because he interprets a natural happening in this way. Moreover, if we say that history raises questions of meaning we can see that this also leads on to further interpretation which seems to depend on something which history alone cannot supply. The Bible goes beyond what the scientist may perceive in nature but also beyond what any historical techniques may provide. The new meaning may be deeper or simply the poisoning of superstition, but it is certainly different. The birth of the baby Jesus in Bethlehem, supposing that it were accurately plotted, will not in historical meaning alone lead on to incarnation. Golgotha, the place of the skull, may be identified by eager tourists noting its geological formation but this will not, of itself, lead them to affirm that God was in Christ reconciling the world unto himself. No evidence of an empty tomb will yield the cry of faith, 'He is risen!', although conceivably some searching could throw doubt on the claim. It seems, therefore, that just as we move from apparently meaningless events in nature to meaningful acts in history, so we are compelled to place great weight on revelation and faith.

These, of course, are questions which concern all Christians. Any parent handing on the story to his child is faced by a barrage of innocent questions which must be answered with some awareness of the modern world. The innocence of the modern child is not that of a garden but, rather, a city. The preacher, however, does not simply tell the story, he proclaims it. He may hopefully wish for some simple way in which he can avoid the questions people ask but he can do this only by cutting himself off from the language and experience of modern man. I have said enough to show that there is an anxiety about this. Indeed the anxiety has grown with modern ways to such an extent that the man of faith is tempted to believe that his own experience of God is quite impossible for the man of today. He feels a stranger among people who view his ways as an idiosyncracy carried over from some former days of darkness. Sometimes there are genuine intellectual perplexities with which a man wrestles and at the end of a weary conflict he reaches the conclusion that faith can no more be a reality for him. More frequently a subtle mood is communicated which makes faith meaningless. God slips out of life like a man leaving a room full of people, and no one notices that he has gone. The position is aggravated for the preacher because he proclaims in public a faith which has been lost. I have often witnessed people changing from belief to unbelief without being able to detect when the transformation took place. I suspect that if philosophical and radical writers constantly assert that no modern man can believe this or that or that it is impossible for twentieth-century man to have faith in God, then a torpor descends on the people until they are roused to a renewed faith, or faith in some modern idolatory. It is not intellectual struggle which makes the peasants of Brittany lose their faith on the journey to Paris or students from some provincial town leave their faith on the train before they arrive in London. It could be argued that a faith so easily lost was never held, but this is a harsh judgment which does not recognize how readily we are all willing to be conformed. It needs time to observe what is taking place in the experience of men and women, but most of us are content to take the rule of the day as the measurement of eternity.

The anxiety of the preacher encourages him to hope that radical questions may be answered by conservative assertions. There are pressures here, too, and Christians are sometimes driven closer to one another so that they celebrate an intimate faith rather than the redemption of the world. The only alternatives seem to be either a surrender to the mood of the times or a deliberate, exclusive resistance. I do not believe that this latter alternative should be despised. Particularism in Judaism preserved much for later ages, however lamentable it was as an abiding attitude. The truth is that the destruction of ancient authorities which were regarded as primary has thrown the church into confusion. Whether it is the church or the Bible which is being doubted it is clear that we are faced with the question of the reality of faith in God through Christ. If the New Testament, despite some modern apology for its historical validity, is no longer the primary authority, where does this lead us? If the church, as with Roman Catholics, can no longer speak the final authoritative word, what way is open to us? How is the preacher to proclaim the gospel without the trumpet having an uncertain sound?

It may seem strange to claim that it is in this situation that the New Testament can live again. Whether this will happen soon or late depends on God and the faith men put in him. If there is no God to whom the man of faith can respond, then that will be the end of the matter. But it will need more than sociological pressures to destroy this experience. The living tradition from the God of Abraham, Isaac and Jacob; the faith of Israel pulsing with painful life under the hammer blows of the world; the people of God born in travail and witnessing to the continuing life of Christ are not destined to end in a faithless whimper. Paradoxically, there are men who confess their faith when it is said that the experience is not possible to modern man. No man, least of all the preacher, should feel that he is left alone sulking under a juniper tree. The experience of the man of faith is multiplied many times more than he can count in every age and nation. The New Testament gospel plays its sad but triumphant song on strings which seem so fine and delicate that we tremble lest they should be broken. From the beginning the gospel is full of appalling risks. It is a story entrusted to common men about a fluttering life that could not be stopped in the cradle, on the cross or at the grave. The faith, like God from whom it comes, has its dwelling place with men. The risk taken by God, as Wheeler Robinson used to speak of the incarnation, is an abiding hazard with men. The story lives by being told; it will triumph by being proclaimed.

9

Dying to Live

What, then, is to be proclaimed? It would be well to come to this question with a warning. We are not speaking of something which may now be proclaimed because some scholars assure us on certain facts in the Bible story. We could suppose this only by being faithless to what we have received and insulting to those who have gone before. Just as a belief in God which is confined to people with a mastery of logic and a gift for argument must be rejected, so the declaration of the faith cannot be restricted to scholars or those acquainted with their findings. There are disciplines where a limitation of this kind is necessary. But in a faith which claims to be catholic it would be disastrous.

The people called Christians have always had to rely on someone. At the beginning there were those who told the story because they were in a position which enabled them to know about it. It was not a question of choosing a few people who had a gift for story telling. They were the ones who had witnessed the events and heard the parables. Even Paul after his wanderings in Arabia found it necessary to drop in at Jerusalem to have some conversation with Peter. He had no time for those who simply made up a gospel. When the oral tradition became a written story, Christians were compelled to depend on the reliability of the authors. Yet, again, with the early need of translation it is quite obvious that the new language of the gospel depended upon gifted translators whose work has been multiplied as the faith advanced into new territories. So our fathers, even when some were familiar with Hebrew and

Greek, learned to accept what they themselves could not have achieved. It is also understandable that there were many who began to comment on the story told and this has gone on throughout the centuries. Sometimes there was a piety which refused to question or was incapable of questioning radically and the modern age in biblical scholarship is distinguished by its willingness to be more searching in its inquiry. It would seem unwise and ungrateful to ignore the results of careful scholarship or to refuse to test the tradition by it. An unexamined gospel is no more commendable than one which has been invented.

It is necessary, then, for the modern preacher to know that he is dealing with the New Testament faith. He has entered into an apostolic succession and preaching must likewise be apostolic preaching. He does this by understanding the nature and substance of the apostolic message and in this he can be greatly helped by the scholarship which he has also received. It is not, however, necessary for him to be a scholar. In order to be a preacher he must have certain gifts, including one of articulate speech, but he need not be a man vastly acquainted with the language and customs of the ancient world. On the other hand it will be a benefit if he is not stupid or inclined to handle the New Testament text in a silly and irresponsible manner. Even if people consider him to be an ignorant man he will not be without power if he is steeped in the message of the New Testament and in the faith of his fathers. Indeed, if this be a mark of his station it will not be easy to dismiss him as an ignorant man. He may be dubbed ignorant only when he is presumptuous and arrogant about a faith which both requires and demands humility of mind and heart. But there is no reason for a little or much learning to make a preacher mad or ineffective. If he cleaves to some particular manifestation of the church to the exclusion of all others it matters little whether he is described as a radical or a conservative. He may cheerfully produce his own creeds or be stubbornly literal and demanding about ancient ones but if either of these exercises severs him from Christendom he would do well to pause and reflect. Yet apostolic preaching is always contemporary. In addition to the forms which are rooted in the New Testament and in the history of the church, there must also be the ever creating spirit which reveals a living relationship with contemporary life. That is the character of the faith we preach. It is not antiquarian nor modern. It is eternal and contemporary.

The preacher who finds the Apostles' Creed a stumbling block may consider that he has escaped from an awkward predicament. He will breathe freely and prepare to offer the people his own inspired intuitions. This, I fear, cannot be allowed. No man can repeatedly transgress the rules of the game and still be regarded as a member of the team. Since we are living in enlightened days it would be improper to silence him. He has liberty to speak as he pleases and providing he has gifts of personality he is not likely to feel deprived even in his chosen vocation. The point is clear that where liberty of interpretation is already considerable a preacher either stands within the apostolic lineage or he does not. His views may be enlightened and admirable in many ways but one has a right to expect that if he is a Christian preacher there should be some recognizable link with New Testament faith and the church to which he claims to belong.

Let us suppose that loyalty to a tradition makes it unlikely that a minister will lead the congregation in saying the Apostles' Creed. This will not enable him to escape from the question of belief. Presumably if he has a belief then he must believe something which can be expressed, however inadequately. It is quite possible that creeds as such do not appeal to him because he knows that their history is not altogether a happy one and he is aware that they have sometimes been imposed in inhuman ways. But a mistaken zeal about the nature of a covenant does not, by any means, affect the declared substance of the faith. It will be appreciated that I am not tempted to urge a literalism about the Bible or anything else related to the faith. Yet I am sure that the sources of the Christian way cannot be blocked without drying up the river. So I am content to recognize the validity of C. H. Dodd's outline of the contents of early Christian preaching. The references in Paul's letters and the record of Peter's speeches in Acts have a dignified antiquity and Dodd believes that they take us somewhere within the first decade after the crucifixion. In these we find the kerygma stated – the fulfilment of prophecy; the early life of Jesus; the crucifixion and resurrection; the exaltation of the Lord; the gift of the Spirit and the universal judgment of Christ. There is enough there to believe or not believe. It is historical, redemptive and catholic. Now, of course, it is possible to dismiss the apostolic kerygma claiming that it has no validity in history and no contemporary reality. I am simply saying that if a man is a Christian preacher these themes will be an essential part of his message.

The preacher will do well to remember the apostolic kerygma. Without it he will be in danger of proclaiming a Christian faith which has little to do with Jesus and of being imprisoned by the moods of his own personality even when he imagines he is most free. In this connection it is significant that Bultmann went to some pains to warn that a man must be careful not to claim that he is speaking to God when in reality he is only speaking to himself. God cannot be confined within the believer and although he is apprehended by faith, he exists apart from it. In the service of worship both in word and sacraments it would be folly to forget this. Yet although we express belief in this way – recollecting the outside as well as the inside – I doubt whether this declaration can be the best door for the modern man in his groping and perplexity. I am constantly reminded that modern man is largely untouched by the kerygma partly because he does not hear it and partly because secularism has made it hard for him to hear even when he is within sound of a voice. In this situation it is perilously easy for the preacher to indulge his own impatience and pride in a 'take it or leave it' attitude which shows none of the compassion so marked in our Lord.

The door for modern man is the door of experience interpreted by faith. The experience is personal. That is, it knows of God and the life of man by something other than second hand. A man who speaks of God always does so in the light of some understanding he has of himself. Indeed it would be difficult for a man to do otherwise unless he expresses his faith only in terms which he has picked up from others. This may be expedient for a time but it proves worthless when the foundations begin to shake. In stating this position it is important to remember once again that such a personal experience is not divorced from the community of believing people nor from the apostolic word. A man who deceives himself by imagining that his experience is strictly individual has not begun to understand himself nor the nature of the community of man. Individualism which runs riot has wrought much havoc in the church and in the world. A man who thus relies on the door of his own personal experience cannot truly evade the community nor can he be released from the responsibility of his relationship to dogma. The experience of men will have a unity within it like the binding power of covenant. There is, of course, also a good deal in experience which divides and one of the first steps to self-understanding will be a recognition of what it is that alienates and corrupts. But it must be emphasized that personal experience will lead to certain accepted expressions of belief, if there is any sense at all in human life, and it is in this sense that we have welcomed dogma.

Any minister will know that there are moments in the lives of people which transform a disparaging view of human nature. Even when evil prevails and sermons become full of foreboding and gloom there is a word or deed which shatters the most impregnable, pessimistic citadel. Just when a preacher has pictured greed and inhumanity, as in a time of war, some little man squanders his life with incredible courage so that the universal dirge has to be revised because of this one man. Caring not for himself or whether there are people to witness his action, this unknown man gives his life for others when he could have preserved it. Or, as I saw in my youth, men who can boast of no high virtue rush to offer themselves for the sake of a companion when they hear the pit-top hooters scream, warning of an explosion deep in the earth. Or, again, here is a person who dedicates his life to caring for the children for whom he suddenly became entirely responsible when his wife died. So we could go on and frequently if we searched for some avowed faith or church allegiance we should find none. Moreover, people who observe these acts in undistinguished lives feel themselves looking in respect and reverence at what they have seen, feeling the grace and judgment of it within their own lives. It is as though they had caught just a glimpse of the 'eschaton', the ultimate, the real. These moments come not in examples of self-display but always in self-sacrifice which portrays an enrichment of life.

Then again we have seen and heard of people who have been through destroying fires only to emerge after a long travail into the hope and promise of a new life. Where the condemnation of death had been spoken there is born the word of life in times of flood, earthquake and war. There are many ways of explaining this rebirth and the reasons are not common to all, but to see a country broken in pieces and then to witness a resurrection is all a part of the incredible human story. It is notable that the supreme example here is in Israel, although many peoples have similar stories to tell. The significance of all this is that sin and alienation, with atonement, death and resurrection, are patterns that run through human life. There are long tracts of life where these experiences, both personal and national, are hidden. No trace can be found of any meaning or purpose nor yet anything which makes a man pause as though he were in the presence of the miracle of God's love in the world. Yet the reality of these experiences cannot be doubted. I have referred anonymously to occasions of this miracle in the lives of ordinary people. It would be possible to multiply this in the stories of well-known men and women and outstanding periods in history. I resist doing this simply because it will be well for the reader to reflect on such moments known to himself and within himself which were never recorded in any book or newspaper.

Now these experiences which may be rare – and usually are – but which beckon a man's life beyond what seems meaningless and pedestrian, are one side of the miracle. The other side is that when we look at the New Testament story the signals of light burst through in parables of the kingdom where the darkness is momentarily broken. The story is so framed that all is related to the death and resurrection of Christ. Karl Mannheim says that we choose our approaches to given situations by certain decisive experiences which give direction to life. If this is so then we can be sure that the intention of the New Testament writers was to claim the death and resurrection of Jesus as the pattern of what being a Christian means. It seems that the shafts of light which illuminate our self-searching meet, in the story of Jesus, the supreme illustration of what life means. If that is so then it is a miracle which brings an undoubted sense of the presence and power of God. After all, that is what a miracle is and we must not complain if it depends both on experience and on faith. When I was a child missionaries used to tell us that if they showed primitive people a portrayal of the cross and told them the story of how Jesus died, they would respond to the story with great seriousness as though it were already speaking to something deep within them. That is a very simple way of saying what F. W. Dillistone has traced so magnificently in *The Christian Understanding of Atonement.*[1] Whether it is said simply or unveiled in the rich thought of the ages it merits reflection. After all it could be true.

There have been periods when scholarship has been paraded in such a way that the preacher has become stiff and crippled in his efforts to make the word plain. Constantly glancing over his shoulder he has found it difficult to move himself or the people. But when scholarship is absorbed, the mind and imagination become free. Scepticism in biblical criticism must also be critical of itself if it is to escape from falsifying the message. There can be no message where New Testament words are reduced by rigid scholarship simply to an examination of the parts, so that people may discurse freely on the grammar and syntax but be abysmally dull when it comes to interpretation. The man who by reputation knows all about the Bible but yet conveys the impression that it is not worth reading is not a man to be envied. Analysis of any literature may achieve this strange result but it is the more lamentable in literature which is of the people and which speaks to the common life and destiny of all men. This may be seen where preachers talk of the cross and resurrection. They seem to know the background, the ancient customs, all the various words for sin and the shades of meaning in salvation, but the congregation celebrate as though they were in the presence of a skilfully dissected corpse.

Confirmation of this understanding of death and resurrection is not limited to the New Testament story, to experience or theories of the atonement. It is to be found also in the apparently bewildering activity of the church from the beginning. The image which the churches present sometimes threatens to conceal this. I think this is largely because when the churches concentrate on some self-conscious, distinctive image of themselves they reveal a remarkable facility for corrupting the image of Christ. This is usually achieved in ignorant and, possibly, innocent ways. Let us look at the modern church in this connection because that is far enough from the days of the New Testament and near enough to us to be sufficiently revealing of what has taken place. The Roman Catholic church may clutter the sanctuary with all kinds of images, bits and pieces which are supposed to hold some traditional sanctity, so that the wayfaring man may be forgiven if he suspects that there is the worship of a variety of objects. I remember sitting with a small group of priests and ministers watching a film which was meant to display what went on in a Roman Catholic church. The film had been produced with the best of intentions. It was an effort to explain Roman Catholic practices to confused Anglicans and benighted Nonconformists. It seemed that getting into the church demanded a variety of gymnastic bowings and bobbings where progress along the aisles depended upon a complicated esoteric knowledge of what the different objects represented. The Roman Catholic priest sitting beside me could scarcely contain his wrath and made no attempt to conceal his annoyance. He told me that if I entered any modern Roman Catholic church I should be faced with something quite different from the elaborations which were being thrown on the screen before us. Yet I secretly nursed the impression that I had seen something like this film portrayal in a number of Roman Catholic churches. The priest beside me, however, was much aware of Vatican II and the reforms which in his view had emphasized the essentials. These would certainly include, as the heart of the matter, the word and the sacraments and undergirding them the cross and resurrection of our Lord.

At the other extreme, in common understanding, are the activities of the Free Churches. A vigorous Free Church usually has a board announcing to the neighbourhood that it is active and vital. Apart from the Sunday services there are meetings for men and meetings for women and frequently these are divided into separate functions according to age or inclination.

There are youth activities from fellowship and social occasions to quasi-military organizations for boys and girls; there are choir practices, bright hours, ecumenical groupings and anything else which is capable of filling a need. All this has performed a valuable social function but the essential thing is that here is a church fellowship which celebrates in hymns, prayers, Bible readings and sermons the great drama of the death and resurrection of Jesus. From time to time the heart of the matter may be hidden in social activities and historians are able to paint the picture of a lively fellowship which appears to have no worship at all. In this sense the Free Churches have obscured the purpose and true life of the church as successfully as some of the Roman Catholic or Anglican activities. Yet in word and sacraments from the beginning until now it is the death and resurrection of Jesus which has been proclaimed and celebrated in all the branches of the church. Even when the Lord's Supper and baptism are not celebrated, as with the Salvation Army or the Quakers, the theme is still of dying and rising with Christ and all is contained in the story of Jesus.

That which receives common support from experience and the New Testament, from the theories of theologians and the history of the church and which is celebrated in the central acts of Christian worship cannot easily be overlooked. If it is neglected it simply means that an institution called a church has ceased to be a church however effective it may appear to be. I must be blunt about this. I believe that the act of preaching, the proclaiming of the message where God acts by the word to bring dying men to life again, is the soul and centre of it all. We make desperate efforts to manage without the word. Let us leave the preaching of the word, we say, and we sponsor programmes of education, music, social service, stewardship and, where growth moves apace, we point to our successful promotion and planning. There are pastors and preachers who become slaves of a system yet boast, particularly in the USA, of growing statistics, huge budgets and God knows what else. By all means let us observe the sociological significance of this enterprise but where the word and sacraments are lost in decent or indecent obscurity there can be no living church.

The position we have reached in this chapter may be seen

as a narrowing of the full flow of Christian proclamation so that it should be given direction and force. Beginning with apostolic preaching and its expression in the Apostles' Creed we claimed this tradition for ourselves. Although the dogmatic insistence on the interpretation of the faith was viewed with suspicion we nevertheless recognized the essential place of dogma. We argued that the door for modern man is through experience, not because all experience is wise and creating but because, with all its perils, there is no other door. Research in the nature and psychology of man can help us here, but the point need not be given unnecessary sophistication. It may be understood in terms of the traditional claim that man is *capax Dei*, i.e. not that the finite can contain the infinite but that man, despite rebellion and sin, is sufficiently akin to God to be able to discern his action and to enter into communion with him. Moreover, there are flashes of light in the lives of common people which enlighten the darkness in which preachers are sometimes tempted to dwell. The illustrations of this are to be seen in a simple liturgical formula which pictures, in action, death and resurrection, dying in order to live, self-denial leading to self-affirmation or sacrifice leading to fulfilment. These experiences are not simply individual, for they are found in the person and the community. We then saw that the supreme event, in the New Testament and throughout the interpretation of the church, was found in the death and resurrection of Jesus Christ. This is what is celebrated in the worship and proclamation of the church. Without this there may be a useful and helpful community but it could not properly be described as a church. The miracle, rooted in faith, is the meeting of responsive human experience with the event which Christians claim stands at the centre of history and the world.

10

The Kingdom by a Word

It will seem to some that in the previous chapter I have managed to achieve what I previously condemned. The claim that death and resurrection is the central theme to be proclaimed could be viewed as a minimal definition or a way of reduction. But I have no ambition to reduce the Christian gospel to trivial or dogmatic proportions. The death and resurrection theme is not a contraction because it contains limitless possibilities. The door is not shut in some false claim to finality. The door is opened into the eternal world.

Now it is true that death and resurrection is a common theme both in the ancient and modern world. That is the very reason why it becomes the door of experience. If it were restricted to one faith or could be understood only by a specialized group then, of course, it would be a serious disadvantage in any gospel which is offered to all men. It might be supposed that the message could be given as something entirely foreign to human nature, injected, from without, into some part of man's being. I prefer to believe that there is already the capacity for kinship between God and man so that it is possible for men to receive what is proclaimed. We learn of goodness, of love and of mercy because already there are rumours, as well as perversions of these in men and women. This is putting mildly what is expressed magnificently in the incarnation and in the Pauline view of Christ in you the hope of glory. Moreover we have not simply been formulating general truths but insisting, as the Christian faith certainly does, on Jesus as God's word to men.

It is significant that when we start with the death and resurrection experience we soon find ourselves moving through that door on to wide horizons. Indeed if I were driven by limited time and a sense of urgency to gasp in one word the message of the New Testament I should speak the word 'resurrection'. In the same way a Jew might proclaim his own faith in the one word 'exodus'. The Christian word is 'resurrection', not, as L. P. Jacks used to say, 'immortality'. But once the word 'resurrection' is spoken within the context of the faith and by a Christian there follow questions about the nature of the life, the death, the person of Christ, his relationship to God the Father, the kind of salvation he offers and how the world is redeemed. You will have the apostolic kerygma, the Apostles' Creed and the whole world on your hands before you know where you are! I have attempted to come to some of these questions in the Bible story with a respect, though not an improper reverence, for the work of scholars. I found it necessary to accept the integrity of scholarship and I have traced in outline something of the wavering course. This does not mean that we reach a contrived unanimity about the Bible or the history of the church. There are conservative scholars and radical scholars and there is the faith of both. If they wish to spend time hurling abuse at each other then we must accept it as an illuminating illustration of the nature of man. At best they will correct, reprove and encourage one another in the pilgrimage of man; at worst they snarl and bite over the Bible like dogs with a bone. It is no service to truth or the life of faith when the views of another are twisted in order that they may be caricatured. When Cardinal Heenan,[1] in dulcet tones, tells the radio-bound British public that Bultmann opened the way of scepticism about the miracles, hinting that he taught that the feeding of the 5,000 could be explained by the issuing of something like food-vouchers, he may raise a breakfast-table giggle. But Heenan is ignoring the apostolic warning about tickling the ears of people and I can only pray that he will make a good repentance.

When we enter into the apostolic heritage and claim this gospel as the life by which we live, we then have to ask what is to be done with it. It is a reflection of our times that we ask this question at all. Although people now hear more words than ever before, through radio and television, the church often gives the impression of despising speech within the act of worship as though it could be used only for endless palavar. There are different ways of doing this. In desperation preachers cut the sermon, receiving warm congratulations for this act of understanding, and resort to dialogue, happenings and visual aids. This insight is not as modern as it seems. Christmas, for example, has revealed over many years that a manger and a few carols will draw more people to an evening service than any preaching of the word. Relatives and friends of all who participate turn up for a celebration where they are confident there will be no declared meaning about what is being done. It is like a gorgeous presentation of the eucharist where people ask no question about meaning because they like the colour and the sound. Then again there is the plea for a practical application of the Christian ethic. I asked a young man, recently, who was about to be married whether he went to church. His reply sounded like a gratuitous insult to a preacher although it was spoken in innocence. He simply looked at me and said, 'No, my religion is a practical one.' He belonged to a multitude of people who do not object to an occasional celebration such as a wedding, but who like to feel that while others talk they get on with the job at hand. I find also that there are a good many self-confessing Christians who rarely attend worship but who never miss an opportunity of talking about 'belief'. At my church in Bloomsbury we have many visits from Members of Parliament and people in public life who offer all kinds of solemn views about the application of the Christian ethic but would regard listening to a sermon as an indecent interference with their busy lives. Yet again, I have noticed how some of my most garrulous friends have joined the Quakers, not because the meeting gives them an opportunity to talk but because they claim to prefer silence to a sermon.

These are but a few of the attitudes I have detected in the modern mood. There are many others. Yet primarily they seem to be influenced by visions and dreams rather than the word. They tend to prefer action, however random, rather than speech although they speak much about action. They admire a good image of the Christian faith, feeling that this may be seen in Jesus but not in the church, and only in other people when they are outside the church. Many of them, like the people who have left the chapels of Wales, feel no shame that they no longer follow the ways of their fathers but would be insulted if they were accused of being unchristian. They respond readily, if fitfully, to what they consider to be original ideas and there are preachers who foolishly feed them on this illusion. I remember as a student clambering down the gallery stairs after Dr Sangster had been preaching in Brunswick, Leeds, hearing a fond worshipper say: 'I like Dr Sangster because he makes me think . . .'

Now far be it from me to pass a harsh judgment on any of these admirable sentiments. Visions, dreams, action, new ideas, all have an important place in the story of man but, as with Paul Tillich in his view of cultural arts, I believe that in worship there is a famine of the word. To insist that the word has an essential place in worship will seem a strangely reactionary view to the minds of many people. They will not find it difficult to speak of Christ as the word of God although it may not be easy to form any clear idea of what that means. The sense of mystery, however, can encourage meditation and wonder. But to speak approvingly of the proclaimed, the preached word will seem an improper attitude. For modern man the sermon has been divorced from the word in a way in which the Reformers could not have imagined. As with marriage problems the trouble is nourished by the two parties. The preacher has come to believe that he merely fills up a space, in the order of worship, which gives him much anxiety and the people feel that the day of the prophet came to a stammering end long ago.

I must admit that this plea for preaching in the modern world needs some apology. Having been a preacher for a good many years I can well understand that people should consider it a strange way to spend one's life. Is there something peculiar about speech which makes it impossible to find a substitute? If so, what is it that makes speech so important and essential? When someone claims that there is no substitute for preaching I assume he means that preaching is a distinctive form of speech and that its value does not lie in any magical properties but in this particular means of communication and the setting in which it takes place. Is there, then, a special language or will any kind of language do? Hesitations about accepting an approach of this nature can easily be understood. It is said, for example, that there are other and better means of communication and we shall look at some of them in the light of the attitudes to which we have already referred.

The most obvious competitor with the preacher in terms of communication is the media of religious television. It is, I believe, true that television producers would not choose a religious service, with preaching, as the most suitable place for the giving of the Christian message. The trouble is not with this opinion but with the conclusions that are commonly drawn from it. That is, the general assumption that whatever may be done in a church service is still done much better on television. Linked with this is the assumption that the Christian message may be given in ways more effective than words. I spent a number of years in close contact with the BBC and ITA as an advisor to both bodies. I am confident that preaching, as such, is relegated to the most inferior place and because it is thought not to be suited to television it is popularly assumed that it has no vital significance anywhere.

There are some interesting results which arise from the producers' concentration on the idea and the image rather than the message. It frequently happens that those who organize religious television have no living relationship with the church. Indeed it is sometimes supposed that a church member is placed at a positive disadvantage because he is too intimately linked with the cause. The professional skills required can obviously be displayed by an atheist, just as it is not necessary for a man to be a Christian in order to build a church organ or a pulpit. There have also been admirable church caretakers who were not distinguished for their piety. Yet it is remarkable that so many people have been employed, even in influential positions, in broadcasting a faith in which they have no belief.

The BBC has tended to recruit its producers from the clergy although this, in itself, does not guarantee a close relationship with the church. Indeed, there are clergy and ministers who, once they are set free from church disciplines, demonstrate their new freedom by having as little as possible to do with it. The BBC, however, guards against the intrusion of religious bias by inviting non-religious people to chair and participate in the programmes. It may well be thought that if a man takes part in religious programmes long enough he may, like Malcolm Muggeridge, eventually 'get' religion. The record here must be disappointing.

Independent Television often appears to work on the assumption that the best people to deal with religion are those who have no experience of it. Bright, varied programmes may be devised which are submitted to a panel of bewildered, part-time religious advisors. Since most people in this country avoid the dangers of worship it is understandable that the popular programmes will be those which are not too obviously linked with the church or, indeed, with the Christian faith. The logic of using non-Christians will be clear to the intelligent reader. One reason for this curious approach to religion is the fact of competition. If one channel has managed to obtain, at a price, Sir John Gielgud or Sir Ralph Richardson to read the Bible, there is little point in the other offering the Rev. Tom Smith as an alternative. Mr Smith may be scholarly, saintly and enlightened but he suffers from anonymity. Sir John or Sir Ralph may happily murder the prophets in a pleasant voice but it is this voice which will be heard and this face observed. Critical readers will surely understand that there is no point in producing a television programme if no one, other than relatives, is going to look at it. The aim, then, is to guarantee viewers and it has long been established that the most consistently popular religious programmes are those which offer hymns, sacred songs and solos. The producer for these highlights of British religious celebration needs the qualities of a chef. The ingredients are – well-loved hymns, moving ballads, romantic scenery or familiar chapels and entertainers touched by an appearance of devotion. The whole thing is then spiced by a professional footballer or a pious MP. Ministers may be used to take the mixture out of the oven, muttering the benediction as they do so.

Let it be admitted that those responsible for religious television have a difficult task. There are many examples of programmes within the limitation of the medium which portray the things that belong to Christian compassion, care and love. Yet it is, alas, more impressive to hear a prominent politician claim that, say, Reinhold Niebuhr changed his life – however poor the evidence may be – than to watch a theologian interpreting Niebuhr. The problem in all this is the image. A self-conscious attractive image of the church or the Christian faith is woefully prone to deceive. It can so easily appear to be an effort by earnest people to present themselves in an attractive light. Perhaps we shall appreciate the problems of the poor producer if we look at the image in Isaiah: 'He hath no form nor comeliness; and when we shall see him, there is no beauty that we should desire him . . . (Isa. 53.2).

It seems to me that we must always bear in mind that the image to be presented cannot be caught by any self-conscious or contrived performance. If a producer is an atheist attempting to present in the best possible way the faith of others he may succeed where his work is marked by an open integrity. If he is a Christian he must remember that he is not merely to display in an attractive light the cause he is tempted to propagate. The perils in either course are sufficiently obvious. It is for this reason that the essential message of the Christian faith is communicated when the intention is not blatantly thrust upon the people. The communicator is reflecting something which is beyond himself and which was not initiated by him. This may be the reason that a sermon on television looks too much like an improper frontal attack. It savours of speaking at people as though one were espousing a cause as in an aggressive political broadcast. I think there are serious problems facing any preacher who is giving the message on a mass medium and television is much more difficult than radio. Yet the word has more reality and greater possibilities even in this medium than is normally recognized. My main point now, however, is that religious television is not a modern substitute for preaching even in a televised service. It multiplies the temptations which have always pursued the popular preacher. A little anonymity would be a cleansing experience but this is exactly what a mass medium cannot for long endure. There are rare occasions when the power of the word breaks through. I recall one in which a woman in Northern Ireland spoke of a murder she had witnessed when she found herself trying to bring comfort to a young, dying soldier. She simply spoke with great sadness of the thing which she had seen, of how ugly and brutal it was. The love, compassion and judgment in her words recalled a forgotten humanity. There have been occasions, too, when some well-known person has touched the heart of things, speaking not as the official representative of some institution but as though the words came from another, fairer realm.

Another means of communication popular with many people today is the belief in action as a substitute for speech. Where Hegel spoke of ideas as the creating force and Marx drew attention to labour, the modern philosopher tends to urge action. Marcuse in old age knows what rings bells in the people of today. It is not easy to see that this apparently healthy attitude is not always as wholesome as it seems. The Christian is bound to recognize that the God of the Bible is a God who acts. He influences history, as we have seen, and his action is demonstrated especially in the incarnation. The word became flesh. That in itself should make us realize that words alone can neither do what God purposed nor what man desires to achieve. But the insistence on action is attractive to many because of its randomness. It produces impulses and emotional spasms where continuity seems more and more to rely on the paid professional. It is, I think, significant that action has found fulfilment, in fine weather and foul, excitement and boredom, where there has been a basic belief whether in Christian counties or in Mao's China. It will be well for us to record the enormous will for service which has been fostered in evangelical communities. There may be criticism of some of the methods and of a creeping cultural conformity, but both here and abroad there has been this life-long dedication which has sent a stream of doctors, teachers and missionaries into the service of their fellow men. The driving motive of all this has been not so much a concentration on action as a response to a proclaimed faith in which the gospel has nourished the life. Even in the matter of race relations the evangelical influence was, almost as a by-product, much more effective than that achieved by enthusiasts for the social gospel.

I simply want to make the point that there is a strength in the preaching of the word far beyond the use of words. Since it is not now common and therefore not greatly observed, we should remember how men set themselves under the word, as it was proclaimed, and then set out to live their lives in willing service because of an overwhelming sense of thanksgiving for what they had received in grace and love. If it is said that this is no longer possible, we should at least recognize the reality of it once upon a time. Moreover, we need not be too sophisticated to see that there is a considerable difference between a sporadic response to social service and life dedicated wholly to the needs of others. In saying this I am not trying to argue that only Christians serve others or that they are consistent and universal in their response. But I am saying that where people set themselves under the word, responsively and humbly, we readily see signs of what a new creation can be. It is easy to show the hypocrisy and sloth in Christian churches but the achievements of Christ both then and now abide.

Yet it is also possible that the perils threatening human life today are not so much an absence of moral fervour as an indulgence in moral excess. The kind of passion which turns people in upon themselves producing a terrifying self-righteousness. There is, as Michael Polanyi has shown, a fever for brotherhood and righteousness which makes people deny humanity in the very acts that are meant to create it. Here again the long Christian tradition holds repeated warnings of the madness which frequently occurs in men who have sought to set up the kingdom by inhuman means. The selected word in favour of one's own interests or the ambitions of a party is not at all the same thing as the word in Christ. Preachers, therefore, may encourage race-hatred or revolution as the way into the future but they will do so only by being untrue to the faith they profess. Action, in the sense of activism, may well lead to increasing despair unless the proclaimed faith fulfils itself in love.

While being aware of the dark side of the elusive image and the peril of concentrating upon action, as though it sprang in purity and strength from within, we also need to beware of a proud confidence in original ideas as a source of a preacher's power. It is not difficult to realize that ideas have creative energy. Indeed, it is possible to see the man with an original idea cutting a lonely path for himself until he is joined by some companions who are able to share his vision of life. Eventually the people also capture the new idea and they join in the wake of what has been realized by the few before. But people who put their trust in this rather idealistic attitude to life would probably be better served by some ethical church, if they can find one, or they may be encouraged to attend the lectures advertised in a paper like the *New Statesman.* They would soon find themselves among like-minded people who believe that they are influencing the movement of great events when they are often merely admiring their own cerebral motions. They would also discover that they are enjoying the kind of intimate fellowship which they have frequently condemned in the more modest meetings in churches.

A preacher who has the reputation for distilling new ideas is also prone to this kind of pride. There seems to be nothing to explain his notoriety other than his own gifts. He therefore assumes that he has been chosen, if he can accept so primitive a view of calling, to make Christian theology palatable for today. People who wander into his tabernacle go away expressing astonishment at such remarkable originality. He is then tempted to be original about everything. The windows he provides do not open on to any eternal world for in the act of looking through them the people see through him. I have been in the habit of telling ministers that one of the purposes of a service of worship is to enable people to endure boredom. That is, to encourage people to walk without fainting when they would prefer to fly like eagles. Discreet friends tell me that it is not wise to advocate the benefits of boredom in this way because there is already ample provision for it in most religious services. So let me put it another way. The service of Christian worship, including the sermon, engages familiar things. The discipline demands not that one should introduce novel things in order to make it more interesting but that familiar things should be presented so that they never lose the element of surprise. The eucharist will not be more real if we substitute cakes for bread and a sermon is not improved by speaking of Christ in such a way that he is no longer recognizable because he looks like some contemporary hero or anti-hero. The preacher is not there to impart choice bits of knowledge nor to inspire by his own eloquence. He is there to enable people to meet Jesus Christ, the word, in the God who gives the word. No bright ideas will achieve this. It may not be flattering to the modern preacher to find that his highest efforts are to be found in an abiding gospel spoken by Peter and Paul, but that is the way it is. The living word does not become old-fashioned.

We must now look at the question of language. It seems pointless to urge the importance of speech if there is not some evidence to validate the claim. I believe this may be done in a variety of ways, and although they may not be as convincing as the sceptic desires they certainly help to bring comfort and, I hope, some conviction, to a preacher who uses language so much. The importance of speech is demonstrated as soon as we see the fate of the dumb. The story of Helen Keller won enormous sympathy because people realized that she had been denied most precious gifts. The struggle to find a form of speech where none seemed available is one that any person can appreciate. Even where the possibilities of speech are present there appear to be almost forbidding complications in the way in which a baby learns to talk. There is not only the intricate system of nerves and muscles which must be developed but the patience of the mother who untiringly repeats words and often the same word over and over again. The cry of triumph which greets the first word of a baby shows that speech is an achievement which everyone desires. It is strange, then, that having gained so precious a thing people should pretend that we are better off without it.

It seems, however, that some forms of language are not as effective as others. Not only was Latin used by early missionaries to overcome the deficiencies of barbaric tongues, but some of the greatest achievements of the Reformers, particularly Luther, are linked with the reform of language. Speech was not merely a matter of using words to carry on the functions of society, it was also a way in which thoughts and beauty were appreciated. It roused men to immense feeling, sending them into battle and stirring them to new adventures. From

Demosthenes to Churchill, the power of the word has been felt by the people even when they had a poor appreciation of language. But in Jewish and Christian traditions the word becomes stronger still. The most common way to describe revelation in the Old Testament is by 'The Word of the Lord'. There are, it is true, visions also but there seems to have been a time when the 'seer' became a prophet. Amos, Micah, Isaiah and the whole sweep of prophetic literature, throbbing with visions and dreams, give the word of the Lord where the command and promise ring out in speech. The prophet who speaks in this way is not possessed, as though he were under the control of demonic forces. His own integrity and freedom are respected. Under a great compulsion (Amos 3.8) he is yet capable of struggling with the God who gives the word, yielding to the command because he has been called to the work of a prophet (Jer. 20.9). Jeremiah, especially, argues and wrestles with God, even reproving him because in certain moods the prophet feels he has been left with an impossible burden. But the word, once spoken, fulfils its purpose as though the spirit and the word were inseparable. When God spoke at creation (Gen. 1.3) he emerged, as the Rabbis put it, from a profound silence. He did not view with astonishment the result of the spoken word. He spoke and it was done. The prophets, when offered this divine power, accepted it only with reluctance and reserve.

The distinction between the true and false prophet was not one of native gifts. It was not that the true prophet was eloquent while the false was dull of speech. It was certainly not that the true prophet became influential by smoothing the path to the door of kings. How speech comes alive in new situations is a mystery to which there is no ready answer. It cannot be understood in terms of language alone as though the new language were holy in its vocabulary. Indeed the very opposite seems to be true. A man proclaims what he has seen and heard and his speech becomes a winged language controlled in its flight yet free because it is not maimed by the formulas of former piety. Hebrew becomes the holy language only when the religious leaders were persuaded that the future of the world would be in the command of those who knew the sacred tongue. It may well be that the stubborn hold of Latin and the professed preference for the Authorized Version have the same love for mysterious roots. But in ancient Israel and in the New Testament it is vulgar speech rather than any esoteric tongue which prevails. Mark's gospel becomes a classic, not because of any superior knowledge of language, but because subject and theme take control and the reader realizes that he is in the presence of great things. Paul himself, when writing to the church at Corinth, goes out of his way to condemn those who through ignorance displayed their rhetoric, achieving nothing but cunning speech. There are times when he seems to wonder about his own blunt speech, but a marvellous insight told him that precious things may be carried in earthen vessels. So he told people about the way of God with the world as he saw it and his words were like a flame. And Jesus, rejecting all the songs of the devil, refused to exploit signs and catastrophies. He announced the kingdom by a word.

I think it is impossible to avoid the conclusion that the faith was born and given life by the word. This is not simply because there were few alternatives in those days compared with our more elaborate means of communication. There were, in fact, a large number of alternatives which could well have been used. Religion is rich and sometimes glutted with all kinds of media of revelation. Some of these are calculated to astonish and terrify the people and, in human terms, they have been used very effectively to get a message across. There seems to have been a variety of choices from natural phenomena, seen to be under divine control, to legions of angels appearing at the appropriate time. A description of the media of revelation would become a history of religions. I can but suppose, therefore, that when Jesus announced the kingdom by a word he was doing so because there is something unique about this way. Moreover, when the church, anxious to be with the times, has endeavoured to employ other means the result may be exciting for a time but the end result is dismal, leading to faithlessness and despair. Religious experience divorced from meaning easily becomes incantation. It was no accident when people, reflecting on the cross, found that worship was the response welling up inside them and they celebrated it in the proclamation of the word, prayers, praise and the eucharistic meal. Nor was it fortuitous that at the Reformation the word came into its own after it had been almost lost in elaborations outside the biblical text and the fellowship life of the early church.

We are living through a time when religious language appears to have been sorely weakened because the claims it makes cannot be proven. Thus it has been argued that such language is meaningless and this has produced a severe loss of nerve. Among philosophers and theologians this is understandable and we can well realize that there is little point in using language of this sort if in fact there is no meaning in it. But the loss of nerve extends far beyond those who have wrestled with the problems and who have some knowledge of the analysis. It reduces the power of conviction in those who know simply by hearsay of the doubts that have been expressed. The difficulty here is not so much in the language used as in the reality of faith itself. Although there are ways in which the language of one generation goes dead in another, I do not think that the significance of speech changes. If we are using it to try to describe something that can no longer be believed or an experience which has been exploded, then we shall simply speak into empty air. Speech may stimulate feeling and create a sense of beauty, but primarily it is the way in which one man speaks to another. Personal insight and experience in one confronts the life of another and this, in itself, is of the nature of persuasion rather than compulsion. That is, by the word I speak another may accept what I say but he may not. Logical argument, supposing that the subject demanded nothing more, can be brutal in its demands and there needs to be something of this in religious debate. But the proclamation with which I am now concerned goes beyond this because it is essentially creative. It does not simply rely on knowledge and argument but rather on the enlarging of experience. This is the nature of all speech which deals with an understanding of life and it applies to humanist and Christian. If the spoken word is lost because it deals only with barren experiences then it will meet with an inevitable destiny of death. It will live only if men and women find life in the word. There is a sense in which the word is true whether anyone responds to it or not, but that is simply a warning about any trust in passing things. If the word is true it will, like truth, prevail though it may need eternity to demonstrate it. This, like the incarnation, is a risky business but I am afraid that there is no alternative way. A preacher, then, must speak the word, always mindful of the language of the world from which the faith sprang and the tongue of his own time. If he finds that his language fails to meet the ears and imagination of his hearers, then he must discipline it the more. If it is the faith itself that gains no response then the preacher can but trust his own experience and the tradition into which he has entered through the Bible and the church. There are seasons when the most vigorous and enlightened word falls on deaf ears. I do not think that the preacher can do much about that except to wait in patience – like Bonhoeffer in his prison cell, waiting, yet believing by the constraint of truth that, one day, new life would be born. 'It is not for us to prophesy the day (though the day will come) when men will once more be called so to utter the word of God that the world will be changed and renewed by it.'[2]

11

The Sermon and Worship

Worship apart from the sermon may be beautiful but without meaning. The sermon separated from worship may become an address in which everything depends on the originality of the speaker. Originality is too ambitious a word. The possibility is that the preacher, thus isolated, will repeat *ad nauseam* the themes on which the congregation is already determined. If the inclination is towards a conservative or establishment position then the congregation will be fed with teaching and rhetoric which confirm the people in their tastes. In occasions of emergency the preacher will become a robed Horatio Bottomley defending traditions with synthetic emotion, displaying a flurry of religious stars in his peroration. If the mood is left-wing then the preacher will provide the revolutionary ardour which the congregation desires. They will get their reward. This does not mean that no sermon can ever stand on its own as a true word. It may do this – but not for long. The sermon is set within the act of worship. The drama and the script are both given.

This is not the place to discuss the questions that arise about Christian worship nor the attempts which have been made to trace the history of the call to worship. We should note, however, that worship is a lively subject among certain groups of people. There is a questioning of the language, the validity of the symbols, the relevance, the place of traditional forms and the link with scripture. I frequently find that Free Church fraternals discuss worship, while Anglican ministers show more concern about the sermon. On the one hand there is dissatisfaction with what is regarded as liturgically thin and on the other an impatience with forms which have been inherited. For myself I should summarize the needs in this way. The word 'form' now implies the outward shape rather than the inner reality. Formal proceedings at a Parish Council or Church Meeting are those occasions when the members feel they can arrive late or slip out discreetly before the benediction. They are not regarded as the very essence of the purpose of the meeting. If we then ask, What is the decisive quality which makes worship what it is?, we shall find ourselves in the synagogue and the upper room with two covenants on our hands. We shall be faced with a recognition of God's worth and the acceptable offering which we would bring to him. I do not believe that we should be too rigid or too precious in interpreting these gifts of tradition and faith. Yet if we are celebrating the gift of God there should be an understanding of the joyful new life in Christ.

I remember an Anglican who attended worship at my church in Bloomsbury. This is by no means unusual but on this occasion my particular Anglican friend felt compelled to impart some views on worship. The service, so he told me, had been spoiled for him because the prayer of thanksgiving preceded any prayer of confession. He found it impossible to celebrate in praise before he had been purged by confession. This seems to me to be so precious that it is beyond my understanding. There are people who like everything to be tidy according to some preconceived pattern and sometimes this fastidious approach to worship is controlled by taste rather than any theological understanding. The norms of a society which approves of dignity or informality become more important than a 'form' of worship. Because of this, worship of another tradition is hard to bear and pentecostal worship is viewed with distaste as though it were a celebration of day-trippers. Then, again, I recall preaching at the first anniversary of the chapel at Heathrow airport. The prayers were shared between a Free Churchman and a Roman Catholic. The Free Churchman ploughed earnestly through a variety of written prayers, invoking the Almighty in a fashion reminiscent of the best established traditions. The Roman Catholic poured out a prayer in which he reminded God that there had been a number of unfortunate air accidents and he hoped that a careful eye would be kept on the maintenance and ground staff as well as the pilots. It was like the prayers I had heard at home when God was told about the hazards of working in a coal mine. The interesting thing to me was that the Free Churchman and the Roman Catholic had appeared to exchange their normal, traditional positions.

I do not know what shape things will take in future years but I am sure that in any living church the heart of the matter will be the celebration in word and sacrament of the new life given in Christ. We have seen that from the beginning this pattern has prevailed. Sometimes a growing sophistication has made later generations rebel against what taste suggests is shapeless and lacking in dignity. I would not advocate deformity in worship but it will be well for us to understand that nice celebrations are of no value when the essential 'form' is lost. I Corinthians 14 must look a bit shapeless to many modern worshippers, but Paul makes clear that any drama of which we may speak does not imply a mere rehearsal of past events. His mind is reaching out to the future, looking into the coming week and listening to the promises of grace. The gifts of repentance and forgiveness are already challenging the hearers to go on living in the light that shines on the new way. This is what makes Sunday worship so strong in power to those who are responsive to the new creation. The day of light, the day of creation and recreation, the day of resurrection and the Holy Spirit – this one day, so rich in meaning, turns the act of worship into the path of faith and hope.

Now the importance which Paul gives to speech, and the different forms of speech within worship, is emphasized in a variety of ways throughout the story of the church. The renewal of worship and continued acts of reformation are a witness to this struggle so that the word and sacraments should not be roughly separated. Not only is this true of the Reformation but it can be seen in modern movements in the Roman Catholic and Orthodox churches. When I have preached in Roman Catholic churches I have often been surprised at the unusual liberty given to the time of proclamation. It is not pushed into a space in the order of worship as though it were a generous concession to the peculiar ways of a Free Churchman. The presiding Roman Catholic priest has tended to encourage the proclamation because his people are hungry for the word. It seems as though it is indecent to confine the Holy Spirit to some brief period of measured time. This, too, has its perils but it is a welcome revolt against habits which are accustomed to treating the sermon as an embarrassing interlude in the liturgy. We know, too, that the Russian Orthodox church has given much more prominence to the sermon in recent years. So much so that the State 'ministers of religion', as they are ambiguously described, who pay some official attention to what is being done in the churches, complain that there seem to be no services without a sermon. This official state suspicion of an act which gives meaning and which proclaims the faith should be a salutary warning to those who in smoother times are ready to reject it. My own memory of some time spent in Russia is of a people who crowded the places of worship as men being offered food long denied.

But it is the setting of the sermon within the act of worship with which I am now concerned. As far as I know neither Roman Catholic nor Orthodox churches are surrendering their liturgies. They are letting the people know what their traditional forms and ceremonies mean and are strengthening them both by experience and the Bible. The main reason for insisting on the word and sacraments, together, is that worship is the experience which precedes any theological expression. When we put credal formulations and theology first we are soon lost either in a maimed liturgy or, what is perhaps worse, in an intellectual presentation of the faith. The desk and tutorial gown become symbolic of instruction and knowledge and the act of worship is coldly cerebral. These developments can only arise when people are so removed from the experience which they celebrate that they give the appearance of having forgotten it. This is undoubtedly one of the reasons for the present lively interest in a pentecostal faith where people long for contemporary life rather than an academic interest in ancient events. It is notable that the new interest in the Holy Spirit is by no means confined to simple and uneducated people. Men of academic achievements, particularly in the Roman Catholic church, have shown rare excitement about the faith when, like Lazarus, they have been released from the binding grave-clothes. The present concern with pentecostalism could run into the kind of corybantic excess which previous generations have witnessed. It is here that theology must fulfil its true role in relation to worship. It must control and discipline the act of worship because men sometimes indulge in wild and wayward ways attributing their extravagances to the Holy Spirit. The New Testament itself speaks of the Holy Spirit with reserve until the experience is baptized into the death and resurrection of Christ.

The preacher who stands within a form of worship, grounded in the word and sacraments and open to the abiding inspiration of pentecost, is not likely to spend time enjoying his own pet themes. That is, he will not find his speech running in well-worn grooves according to his own inclinations nor according to the moods of the people to whom he ministers. The setting of worship will remind him constantly that he is dealing with the faith of the God of Abraham, Isaac and Jacob, the God and Father of our Lord Jesus Christ. The Christian year, providing it is not allowed to be a chain, will give the marvellous rhythm of the great festivals bringing into living remembrance the drama of salvation. This abiding life in worship, expressed in liturgy and the Christian year, is particularly important in an age where there are attempts to reformulate the doctrines of the church. The sermon may well be probing and adventurous but it will be good for the preacher and the congregation to celebrate within a covenant which belongs to the ages. On the one hand, as we have seen, worship may be debased by such a concentration on 'liturgism' that the meaning and interpretation are lost in ceremony. On the other, there can be such a casual approach to the act of worship that it appears to have no significance until the time comes for the children's address or a talk to the adults.

It will be clear by now that worship is not something which may be thrown together by the passing moods of a group of like-minded people. 'Happenings', as we saw in an earlier chapter, may have some occasional value but as a diet for the people they will neither nourish the Body of Christ nor give glory to God. The spiritual life which is centred only in feelings will not build abiding belief because it has no foundation in the eternal gospel.

In Nonconformity of the last century a heavy burden was placed on the minister. Since he served in a separated church he was exposed to temptations which might otherwise have been avoided. There is a sense in which his position in the church had a long pedigree. He belonged more to semitic models than to the church organizations which were based on Greek and Roman ideas of government. It is not too fanciful to picture him as the leader, called and chosen because he had the charisma of leadership. Like his distant predecessors he could not rely too confidently on his calling because his words and deeds were open to criticism every day. He retained his position only if his qualities were such as to be recognized by his people. It was necessary, both for his own peace of mind and security, that he should be able to carry the people with him in his decisions. A discontented minority must be converted by influence or persuasion. The earlier leader had an advantage over the minister because when persuasion failed he could eliminate a minority by his own chosen means. In this situation there were separated ministers who built strong churches which seemed to have little to do with the one church, the Body of Christ. They felt compelled to rely upon their own individual gifts and sometimes the effect was lasting, but frequently the church became a social club or an evangelical stronghold. It would, I think, be wrong to condemn the man of gifts as though he should disappear into some anonymous order. It is significant that Jesus, too, had to carry his disciples with him and that the only one who turned against him stabbed him in the back. Moreover there was much argument about leadership in the early church which was complicated by family relationships as well as any claim to apostolic succession. The conclusion arising from this is not that the charismatic leader is a primitive nuisance but that his gifts belong to the whole church just as the gospel is for the whole man. There can be no doubt that the malady which has afflicted Nonconformity came because of the sundering of word and worship. Sometimes it nourished the giants of the pulpit who had great influence and sometimes it spoke to all sorts and conditions of men in ways which others envied. But the success was a temporary thing and where there was no outstanding successor the church, too, seemed to have died.

People who belong to other traditions must not suppose that Nonconformity, and Congregationalism in particular, were founded upon the shaky foundation of a charismatic leader who by fair means and foul retained his position until old age and death brought his reign to an end. It cannot be denied that there were many examples of this strange way of commending the gospel. But a similar reliance on individual leadership can also be seen in the history of other traditions. In these the leadership rested in administrative gifts or social influence rather than in preaching but they are not any more commendable. It is clear that in any living church the people of God must seek to express the unity and the purpose which belongs to the Body of Christ. Originally the Congregational principle recognized this essential unity. Compelled by circumstance to be separate there was yet a high view of the church. This meant that, although there were different functions within the church and that some were marked by proclamation and pastoral concern, each member was responsible to God for the fulfilment of his will. These people were not misled into believing that, any man's judgment is as good as the next or that every Christian has a right just to speak his own mind in democratic debate or that, alternatively, the members could delegate the witness to others who would do it for them. They were not democratic in the sense that majorities count while minorities are dispensable. As far as they were concerned every Christian is responsible to Christ so that his sovereignty may be realized – 'God's community knows no head but Christ; no other can be endured.' The theme was always the supremacy of Christ, the head of the Body, rather than any emerging sense of the rights of the individual man. Indeed, they were convinced that personal integrity and rights would be preserved only when the life was centred in Christ. It was the paradox of a freedom which could prevail only when all were bound to Christ.

I have no doubt that the Congregational principle had within it the dangers into which all sects easily fall. Like the Puritans there was an elevated thought and experience which tended to ignore the realities in the nature of man. This led either to a retreat into a community of 'saints' or a submission to more common ways of democratic expression. This brings us to the leader, whether it is Ramsey Macdonald or Joseph Parker, who is thrown up by the people because he possesses gifts. The church, unless there is eternal vigilance and responsibility in the members, finds it easier to conform to prevailing political patterns rather than to live by the light it has received. Now this decay from high churchmanship produced disastrous results in the preaching of the word. The old danger which Paul had perceived was evident. Some belonged to this man and some to that as though the church could be parcelled out to individual leaders. The proclaimed word tended to depend upon the favour with which it was received. The people had a mind to accept only what was pleasing to them. A preacher offering an unpopular word, no matter how faithful it might be, eventually found himself rejected by the people with whom he was supposed to be united. Since so much depended upon the communication skills of one man the rest could behave as though they made up a cinema audience. The proclaimed word lacked the one essential thing – it could not become incarnate in a living church.

The way of renewal lies in a worshipping people who are responsive to the proclaimed word and in whom the story of our redemption is celebrated. The congregation in any locality must not pride itself on individual success, nor despair because it is possible only to muster a few. The success in many instances can be explained by the changes in society so that a working-class community may harbour struggling churches whereas a prosperous suburb may breed a thriving church. Faithfulness in the ministry will not guarantee success and it will be well not to be deceived by a growing membership which is conditioned and possibly determined by circumstance. The church is both catholic and local. No catholic church can proclaim its universal mission if it is removed from what are euphemistically called the grass-roots. No local church can be catholic if it depends upon something other than the word and sacraments for its existence. There are no roots other than grass-roots which give the promise of growth. Ecclesiastical administrators sometimes talk as though getting down to the grass-roots were a remarkable condescension. They deceive themselves. The grass does not grow in ancient or modern office blocks and if any were observed in some obscure corner it would soon be uprooted. It should cause no surprise that the catholic church must be expressed in local situations because this is the way of the gospel. It speaks of a particular community and one man. The strategist might imagine that Rome would have been a better place for incarnation than Bethlehem; that the Gentiles, being greater in number, were more promising than the Jews as a chosen people; that love should be offered in general propositions rather than through particular acts; that it would be better to have many books, not one book; a banqueting table for all rather than supper for a few and a cross in the sky rather than a crude bit of wood on Calvary's hill. The gospel not only begins with the particular in order to move on to the universal. The particular abides. This means that a catholic church cannot forget the dominical word about the two or three nor can the two or three act as though the gospel were meant only for them. Any local church is related to every other local church and the bond is in the word and sacraments and the ministry by which they are fulfilled. There are, of course, confusing arguments about the validity of ministry but I now simply make the point that the gospel must be earthed even as God expressed himself in the incarnate word.

It follows from this that the proclamation of the word should not too readily be separated from a community of people. The preacher who moves smoothly from congregation to congregation needs to beware of the temptations to which he is exposed. Since I have been engaged in this activity far more than most ministers I am already being warned to speak with caution. Yet I know that it is deceivingly simple to descend upon a town where a congregation has been assembled by a diligent local community and then to disappear into one's own hole. The peril holds a dual danger. The preacher speaking in general terms, sometimes with a view to entertain, may be blind to the problems faced by the local community of Christians. On the other hand the people, glad of a change from the local clergy, tend to be ecstatic over a visitor however inadequate his words may be. The evangelist who delights in a roving commission is in the greater peril. I recall an evangelist visiting my church in the early days of my ministry who announced in the vestibule after a surprisingly sudden harvest: 'There! I have won these young people for Christ. Now look after them.' I viewed his enterprise with a cynical eye and I am still unashamed to do so after a number of years. The preaching which builds on a sure foundation is the proclamation to a people whose lives are known and experienced. The select preacher is an occasional luxury. The real work is done by the men who are bound by life and experience with a people. Pastor and preacher share the unity of one whole man. The preacher who rushes from the cattle boats to proclaim the word to responsive strangers is simply escaping from his calling, offering the gospel but by-passing both incarnation and cross.

It is sometimes said that a preacher is not limited to personal concerns in the same way as a physician. The physician, when time allows, asks a series of questions about the history of the patient and explores the ailments and health of his parents. The preacher confronted by a congregation knows that, wherever they have come from and whoever they may be, all suffer from a common ailment so that the prescription can be written and presumably included with the sermon notes before the preacher leaves home. There is some truth in this – but not very much. The preacher often proclaims the message to people he has never met and, in the city, it would be difficult to preach at all if this were not possible. There are two things which save the situation and make preaching of this nature possible and desirable. The first is that although the preacher has not met these particular people he has met others. Sometimes he may give the impression that he has never met anyone. That is, he confronts people only from a pulpit and does not seem to want any closer relationship. But if he has a care for people he will be saved from making a fool of himself and from cold, clinical analysis when he speaks to the unknown crowd. The second saving strand is even more important. The preacher gives his sermon within an act of worship. The worship, from beginning to end, emphasizes relationships. The people pray together and sing together. They speak the Lord's Prayer and approach God with a common, indeed a family, relationship already established. 'Our Father . . .', they say, and having been brought, strangely, together they confess already their relationship with each other. Moreover the whole act of worship is not offered in a vague way to whatever gods may be. It is presented through Jesus Christ as the one mediator. If there be any other mediators these are not mentioned. Prayers and praise are 'through Jesus Christ our Lord' – that is the confession and the glad thanksgiving of the congregation. This possibility of a realized unity in Christ lies at the heart of the Christian message. It is the word which breaks down walls of partition even when most experiences of life portray them in concrete. I think this is one reason why Christians who spend their lives in tiny communities find so much excitement in big meetings and large rallies. They feel the link with unknown numbers of people and realize that the two or three together is not meant to be an excuse for a small attendance at the local prayer meeting. This unity in Christ, however, does not depend on big meetings. Wherever it is experienced it witnesses, as Karl Barth put it, to God's provisional demonstration of his intention for all mankind.

The sermon becomes a living word when it is closely linked with worship. Word and sacraments form an indissoluble unity. The word does not depend simply on any eloquence of speech. The source and life are not contained within the gifts of any particular man. The preacher is not given time to speak as though he were a politician during an election anxious to convey his own qualifications and advance his cause. The preacher is a witness. Like John the Baptist, with elongated forefinger, he points. Moreover, he is in the church and of the church because he believes that the church has a mission to perform. Yet the church does not witness to itself. Always there is the life beyond which is given and nourished by God in Christ. Thus we celebrate in word and sacrament. The Christ who is head of the church is the centre and heart of the universe and the church lives to the glory of God and for the love of man.

12

On Being Relevant

The Christian way greeted the world with a story. The tradition is oral. Indeed many of our problems arise from what was inevitable. The story was put into writing. We can understand that for a long period the writing was defended in excessive terms because the people wished to preserve the purity of the primitive story. This, they said, is the story as it was told and we rejoice that those who recorded it were faithful and reliable. The long discipline of transmitting a story from speech to a book was greater than mortal men could bear so it came to be claimed that they were guided infallibly and the text preserved in its purity by a power which is divine.

There are considerable differences, as we have seen, between this attitude and the exercise of critical scholarship. It is possible for a modern scholar to be wholly destructive. Having come to the conclusion that the faith is simply the creation of weird beliefs of long ago, he may simply expose the way it became accepted by deluded people. Yet most biblical scholarship is not of this nature. It may be said that the modern scholar taking the text which imprisons the word sets out to translate it into a liberated word which speaks to modern man. This is the task which is distinguished by the word 'hermeneutics' and, of course, it is also the work of the preacher although his motives and intention are somewhat clearer. It is the work of making it possible to understand the gospel as it is addressed to modern man. Someone has said that the apostolic kerygma without interpretation of this sort is like having an x-ray photograph with no one to tell you what it means. This is putting the difficulty rather strongly, but we can see that if a man is offered a copy of the Bible in a language he cannot read then he will not benefit greatly from it. It will be well for us to realize that the problem is not merely one of a strange language in the sense of a foreign tongue. The work of translation is much broader than this and it is an essential one if the word is to be proclaimed.

We have traced the way in which scholars have approached their work, making it clear that however distressing the results may be the task was inevitable. We must now consider the preacher set in the modern world with the problems which so many revolutionary changes have brought. This has been our concern all along, but there are some further specific things which need to be said. It is, I think, exceedingly difficult for the preacher today to keep a sane balance between the world to which the gospel first came and the world which moves so swiftly in our daily life and experience. Biblical scholarship often seems peculiarly aloof from the everyday. This is true also of a great deal of scientific activity but here it is not so hard to see that there are results arising from science which affect us all, however little we may understand. Biblical scholarship can become the kind of activity which asserts certain judgments about the past which have no relevance for us. Truth in this sense becomes a kind of theological idol. Karl Barth speaks of the way in which the Bible is not only a monument referring to the past but also a document which has a meaning for the present day: 'The text shows where the road leads, but we have to walk on it at the present day.'[1] Barth, indeed, is surprisingly insistent that the words of the preacher must be relevant to the 'immediate preoccupations of his hearers'. Although it is true to claim that the Bible does not become old-fashioned, many ways of speaking about it deal with subjects which are not now important.

The preacher who is aware of this need and who has been released from biblical idolatory is apt to leap into the modern world with his first sentence. I have read pronouncements on preaching which insist that the sermon should always begin where people are in terms of their lives and their experience of events. Fosdick, by example and advice, used to say that the least the preacher can do is to begin his sermon in New York or Seattle or Indianapolis and not in Jerusalem or Jericho or Ramoth Gilead. There is obvious wisdom in this, and since we have spoken of experience as the door for modern men it would be folly now to say that the preacher should begin with something quite foreign to the lives of the people. Zeal for ancient sites and past customs is not likely to set people ablaze for the faith in the twentieth century. But the method once stated is not as simple as it appears. Certainly it can be followed in so superficial a way that it may lead people either to a grossly simplified understanding of the modern world or leave them stuck in the Slough of Despond. If the preoccupation of the congregation is with the balance of payments or the price of beef, to convince them that a change of government alone will remedy the situation does not appear to be an adequate result of the sermon, however desirable this result might be on other grounds. The preacher, also, needs to be aware that the questions which concern him may not really be the questions people are asking. He needs to know the people well in order to be able to enter into their lives. A similar danger of this popular approach is that the preacher anxious to be 'with it' finds himself enlarging on themes which he fondly imagines to be contemporary but which, for his younger hearers, emerged out of the Ark. The real sorrow, however, is when the sermon never gets to any central point and never touches the fringes of the new creation. It was here that earlier preachers were effective even when later homiletic advice considered them to be mistaken. Believing that the cross should be reached, wherever they started from, they frequently spoke to the situation when they scarcely seemed to be mindful of it.

I have come to the conclusion that the preacher is sometimes able to speak to the congregation most effectively when he begins with the Bible. That is, the Bible view of life and of God's way with men has the capacity of going like an arrow straight to the heart. People clamouring to be fulfilled and to have their needs satisfied are suddenly faced by a word which turns their common values upside down. This is the strength in the parables of Jesus which look like a straight story when you begin reading them and then thrust home a point which pierces complacency. The hearer experiences the encounter between the word of God and himself. Direct face to face speech brings the time, sooner or later, when the word is driven home. It could be argued that the example of the parable suggests that the preacher, too, should create stories which have a similar pattern. This may well be achieved by some but efforts to present biblical teaching in modern dress are not, in my experience, as valuable as one might suppose. There is a controlling power in the story itself, and however it may be applied or adapted the eternal possibility in the story must not be lost. This is certainly true of the parables of Jesus. Different ways of applying them have often proved disastrous, reducing them to trivial little tales.

Although we must begin speaking to people where they are, there is no fixed way of doing this. The essential thing is that the eternal word should not be located in the past nor trivialized in the present. The word spoken *then* becomes the word *now* but it must not be corrupted or cheapened. It should not surprise us that the Bible story has the strength to hold us within passing events, for much the same is true of the myths of Greece and Rome. All great stories have something lasting to say about life. The story with which we are concerned, of Jesus and his resurrection, opens the gates of the kingdom. There is, I believe, no need to fabricate some artificial defence for this claim. You will find over and over again people who illustrate some passionate plea they are making by quoting a New Testament word. That they sometimes do it with some embarrassment matters little. They are simply demonstrating that the Word is relevant. The stories of Jesus are not called parables of the kingdom for nothing.

However we may try to link up with the experience of other people, we should understand that no preacher can get into the modern world simply by trying to jump into it on Sundays. This is not a suitable pulpit gesture. If the preacher knows little about the world and the people in it he is not likely to land on solid ground if he confines his exercise to leaps in the pulpit. Needless to say this kind of occasional gymnastic effort will only succeed in making him appear unnecessarily absurd. I have often wondered about Jesus living a life where he was a friend of publicans and sinners. Those habits of his would not have bothered people if he had not also made claims both for himself and this open way of life. If he had said nothing, presumably he would simply have been regarded as another sinner and that would be that. The space given to this social activity in the New Testament is bound up with what Jesus said about God and the kingdom. In other words it is because this man Jesus, with all his preaching, behaved in such a way that there was a cause for offence. That there were sinners was well known. But that Jesus should speak of their priority in terms of God's kingdom was shocking.

This brings us to another feature of the preacher in the modern world. It is possible for Christians, if they wish, to disappear into the crowd, merging with it and losing any sense of identity. Preachers have some difficulty in doing this because they may be spotted at the races or reading a notorious book even when they feel safe. The commercial traveller would not have told the bishop that story if he had been wearing his gaiters. But most of the time the bishop is the bishop – which is, I suppose, what he is meant to be. It is possible to withdraw from the life of the people and live the life of a Pharisee as though this were the Christian way of doing things. It is also possible so to be identified with all that happens that there is never any individual integrity – that is, a man pretends to be what he is not or that it makes no difference. This business of relationships with people is a peculiarly difficult one and we can see how perplexing it has been from biblical times until now. We know that in the story of Jesus it matters much because when extreme radical scholars go to work on the New Testament they usually emerge with one simple fact about him. Whoever he was and whatever he did and said, we can be sure that he mixed with publicans and sinners.

In many ways it is easier to follow John the Baptist than Jesus. A certain aloofness in social life comes naturally to a man if he spends a good deal of his time hurling judgments at people from the pulpit. The 'no' of Karl Barth when faced with the rise of Nazi power comes easily to some men in the most human situations. It would be well to remember Buber's warning about the separation in logic – only one of two contraries can be true – which is not normally applicable to life. Increasing hostility between peoples who are different whether in race or custom is not the purpose of the gospel, although there is here too a sword which divides. The changes in society, particularly those deceivingly described as permissive, have brought new problems but they have also broken down some of the separating walls of former times. Some Christians have been swift to recognize this, not allowing themselves simply to drift with the tide but viewing the changes with some sense of responsibility. This may be seen in their response to the imaginative writers of our time. Not long ago it was possible to recommend Christian novelists – like Silas or Joseph Hocking – and leave the others on the library shelves. I have heard a number of older men speak of the guilt with which they savoured, secretly, the writings of Thomas Hardy.

The pressures that come on people in modern society are most marked in the realm of politics. This again is a narrow ridge on which the man who seeks to proclaim the word is perched. On either side a gulf, with no room to turn back and a longing for confidence to face what is to be. The temptation of the church has been either to escape from this present world into some comforting and comfortable other world or to jump into politics like a dog into dough. The conservative element, which has prevailed, has nourished many good things in life but it has frequently strengthened the powerful and oppressed the weak. The reaction, so marked in our generation, seems to desire political enterprise as the theological theme and political zeal as the sign of a committed man. This way can but lead to disaster because it is a curious abstraction which ignores what is essential to the life of man in community. It so concentrates on structures that it encourages a mechanical view of human nature. It glorifies functions, forgetting that it is only as persons that men really live. It searches for biological ways of interpreting man, failing to see that a web is being spun to bind the victims who are caught in the threads. There is, I believe, a guilt in the church about those who still work with their hands, a sense that there is no prophetic word to be spoken because of earlier neglect and betrayal. Sometimes the most appalling covetousness is excused through fear of the skeletons rattling in the cupboard. Yet people who believe in repentance cannot spend too long lamenting the past, especially when former ills are exaggerated in order that the present may be viewed in a more favourable light. I agree with Jürgen Moltmann that the need is not to give political systems religious support so much as to be aware of the field, the milieu, in which the Good News is to be given.

We have looked at the history of the proclamation of the gospel in the life of the church, glancing only at much of it but examining the validity of a ministry of the word and sacraments in some detail. I am well aware that there are many, including Christian ministers, who will view with suspicion any reliance on the word in the modern world. It would be foolish not to recognize that some will regard the work as a relic from early days. There are preachers who struggle through the discipline of sermon preparation with no heart for it and with half an eye on the mockers backstage and the indifferent in the pews. These two groups become increasingly hostile in the imagination of a man who has become neurotic about his work. In addition to this, personal relations which were so prominent in the life of a minister and the people seem to have been handed over to various professions who are often looked upon with ill will. It is, of course, fatal to refuse to recognize the insights into human behaviour which have been discovered through psychiatry and sociology. Yet to pretend that either of these is, in itself, a source of inspiration or a substitute for moral values and the life of the spirit is an even more desperate measure. The man who sets himself under the word in order to proclaim it must surely see that, although he can no longer be expected to know all the answers, his vocation demands that he stands at the centre of life. There is an abiding relationship with God, me and my neighbour to which he witnesses.

My final brief word is on 'calling'. No man in his senses would choose to be a preacher. There are too many attractive alternatives which beckon and beguile. If it is thought that any Tom, Dick or Mabel can proclaim the word in their spare time, as an alternative to other hobbies, then that will be the end of preaching. Let preaching become a work to be avoided except by those who believe they must do it. Constraint has been a mark of preaching since Moses became aware of his stammering tongue and Jeremiah felt the fire in his bones. I suppose the way of Christ will stand whether the word is proclaimed or not. But the possibility, now, of men living in the new creation will stand or fall by this witness. A character in one of Brecht's plays cries out, 'For God's sake can't you give us anything but words?' That is a cry from the heart and no preacher and his congregation should forget that the word became flesh and that God has his dwelling among men.

Notes

Chapter 1

1. From an article by Michael Bourdeaux in *The Christian Century*, 10 February 1971.

Chapter 2

1. Klaus Klostermaier, *Hindu and Christian in Vrindaban*, SCM Press 1969.
2. Herbert Butterfield, *Christianity and History*, Bell & Sons 1949, p. 131.
3. Anyone innocent of modern happenings is recommended to read John Killinger, *Leave it to the Spirit*, SCM Press 1971.

Chapter 3

1. Albert Clare, *The City Temple 1640–1940*, Independent Press 1940, p. xviii.
2. Rudolf Bultmann, 'Preaching: Genuine and Secularized' in *Religion and Culture* ed. Walter Leibrecht, SCM Press 1959, p. 237.
3. T. S. Eliot, 'Marie Lloyd' in *Selected Essays*, Faber 1934, p. 419.
4. Liberace, reported in *Jazz Monthly*.

Chapter 4

1. C. H. Spurgeon, *Lectures to my Students*, 1st and 2nd series, Passmore & Alabaster 1885.
2. I wrote about this in a Preface to Douglas Stewart, *Easter is on Monday*, SCM Press 1963.
3. Thomas Jones, *The Native Never Returns*, Griffiths & Co. 1946, p. 15.
4. Ibid., p. 17.
5. Miall Edwards taught philosophy at Memorial College, Brecon.

Chapter 5

1. Alasdair MacIntyre, *Difficulties in Christian Belief*, SCM Press 1959.

2. Ibid., p. 117.

3. D. Martyn Lloyd-Jones, *Preaching and Preachers*, Hodder 1971, p. 271.

4. H. F. R. Catherwood, *The Christian Citizen*, Hodder 1969.

5. *On the Other Side*, Scripture Union 1968.

6. Ibid., p. 67.

7. E. Keri Evans, *My Spiritual Pilgrimage*, James Clarke 1961, p. 97. The reference to Theomemphus is to a poetic work by Williams Pantycelyn, *Bywyd a Marwolaeth Theomemphus* (The Life and Death of Theomemphus).

Chapter 6

1. *Cur Deus Homo?*, ch. 1.

2. The booklets were printed in 1909 in the USA. Two wealthy Californians paid for them to be distributed to pastors, missionaries, theological students and Sunday school superintendents in the English speaking world. Three million copies were circulated.

3. Richard Ackworth, *Creation, Evolution and the Christian Faith*, Evangelical Press 1970, p. 12.

4. Gresham Machen, *The Christian Faith in the Modern World*, Hodder 1936, pp. 43 f.

Chapter 7

1. Theodore Robinson, *History of Israel*, OUP 1932.

2. J. N. Schofield, *The Historical Background of the Bible*, Nelson 1938.

3. J. N. Schofield, *The Religious Background of the Bible*, Nelson 1944.

4. J. N. Schofield, *Law, Prophets and Writings*, SPCK 1969.

5. For a variety of opinions on this question see *The Old Testament and Christian Faith* ed. Bernard W. Anderson, Herder & Herder, NY 1969.

Chapter 8

1. Bultmann, art. cit., p. 238.

2. From the *Collected Writings* (published in German as *Gesammelte Schriften*), quoted by Eberhard Bethge in his *Dietrich Bonhoeffer*, Collins 1970, pp. 361 f.

3. C. H. Dodd is included here because of his book *The Founder of Christianity* (Collins 1971) and because he is indestructible.

4. Wolfhart Pannenberg, *The Apostles' Creed*, SCM Press 1972, p. 47.

Chapter 9

1. F. W. Dillistone, *The Christian Understanding of Atonement*, James Nisbet 1968.

Chapter 10

1. In a broadcast of 12 December 1972.
2. Dietrich Bonhoeffer, *Letters and Papers from Prison*, The Enlarged Edition, SCM Press 1971, p. 300.

Chapter 11

1. Karl Barth, *Prayer and Preaching*, SCM Press 1964, pp. 105, 97.